Marek J. Mura

Henschel
Hs 123

KAGERO

MORE FROM KAGERO

Henschel Hs 123 • Marek J. Murawski • First edition • LUBLIN 2012

© All rights reserved. With the exception of quoting brief passages for the purposes of review, no part of this publication may be reproduced without prior written permission from the Publisher. Nazwa serii zastrzeżona w UP RP • ISBN 978-83-62878-15-4

Editing: **Marek J. Murawski** • Translation: **Marcin Gulis** • Cover artwork: **Arkadiusz Wróbel**
• Color profiles: **Mariusz Tarkawian** • Photos: **Marek J. Murawski's archive, Kagero's archive** • Design: **KAGERO STUDIO**

Oficyna Wydawnicza KAGERO
Mełgiewska 9F, 20-209 Lublin, phone.: (+48) 81 749 20 20, phone/fax (+48) 81 749 11 81
www.kagero.pl • e-mail: kagero@kagero.pl, marketing@kagero.pl
w w w . k a g e r o . p l
Distribution: KAGERO Publishing Sp. z o.o.

The first combat aircraft of the German air force was the Halberstadt CL II, the photograph shows machines of Schlachtstaffel 9, their crews are loading special containers with stick grenades.

One of the German Luftwaffe airplanes that were most praised by its pilots, was the biplane dive bomber and attack aircraft – Henschel Hs 123. It was very surprising since the machine was already outdated and inefficiently armed at the outbreak of World War II. However, its excellent flight characteristics and ability to take punishment led to an unusual situation at the beginning of 1944 when a lot of attack aircraft pilots demanded the modern Focke-Wulf 190 to be withdrawn from their units and substituted by the archaic Henschel Hs 123.

The popularity of the aircraft came from its sturdy construction that proved itself not only in the primitive conditions of the Eastern Front, but also as a strong airframe extremely resistant to enemy fire. The Henschel Hs 123's structure was very durable because its designers did not incorporate complicated electronic and hydraulic systems operating the control surfaces. Their damage often led to a catastrophe of many modern constructions employed by the Luftwaffe. Also, the simplicity of the structure made the maintenance work easier. Despite slow speed, only a few Henschel Hs 123s fell victim to enemy fighters. Its reliable, proven in different conditions engine and excellent manoeuvrability let the aircraft evade potential attacks.

Design and development

The history of the German attack aviation began in the years of the Great War. At the beginning of World War I, the aircraft did not have any armament and their tasks were strictly limited to reconnaissance missions. Gradually, the pilots wanted to be more active over the battlefields. They would often take hand guns, grenades and sometimes even metal darts.

In 1916, the Kaiser's air force detached infantry air force (Infanterieflieger) that, within the Schutzstaffel (defence squadron), used the CL class aircraft (160hp engine, twin seat biplane). For the first time, the close support aircraft were employed by the allies during the battle of Somme in 1916. In his 30 January 1917 report to the High Command of the Ground Forces, Gen. Obst. Alexander von Klück wrote about the actions of the allied air force in the initial phase of the battle of Somme: "The bombing raids and machine gun strafing runs, against our infantry, artillery and supply wagons, conducted from low altitude raised a feeling of defencelessness among our troops."[1]

The first attack mission conducted by the German air force was recorded on 24 April 1917 over Somme, near Graville. On that day, two aircraft from Schutzstaffel 7 were on an escort mission for an artillery reconnaissance plane flying over the front. Hptm. Zohrer, the commanding officer of Schutzstaffel 7, piloting one of the escort aircraft, noticed a German ground unit pinned down by heavy enemy fire. Zohrer left the reconnaissance aircraft covered by his wingman and attacked the enemy positions himself. During the first run, he was greeted by heavy defensive ground fire.At the second run, the enemy defences were silent. The German troops saw their chance and stormed the enemy positions.

The best German attack aircraft of World War I was the all-metal Junkers J I.

Taking into consideration Hptm. Zohrer's report, the High Command of the Armed Forces hastened the development of attack aviation. The demand of direct combat cooperation with ground forces necessitated the installation of radios on aircraft.

In the summer of 1917, a unit of 6 to 9 attack aircraft was attached to every front line corps. The number of aircraft was later increased to 12. The corps command was responsible for training and cooperation with the infantry air force. Every infantry division headquarters had an air force liaison officer attached who acted as an advisor and organized cooperation with attack squadrons.

Attack aircraft were also to direct short range artillery fire (field cannons and mortars). Oblt. Hermann wrote about the first actions of the attack air force: "In the positional war conditions, artillery preparation was most often not sufficient to break the enemy's defences and drive him out of the trenches. Ground attacks lacked additional, highly demoralizing combat means. It came in the form of airmen directly participating in combat. They had excellent results. At altitude of only 50 meters, they flew in front of advancing troops and used their machine guns and grenades to engage the enemy hiding in trenches. They would come back many times and repeat their attacks."[2]

At the end of 1917, because of successes achieved by the German attack aircraft, the allies strengthened their anti aircraft defences on the front line. High losses forced the need for a full breed attack aircraft with better crew protection against ground fire. Such a machine was the twin seat, Junkers J I biplane (Junkers Infanterieflugzeug I – infantry aircraft I) with completely metal structure covered with duraluminum corrugated plates. The pilot and observer seats were fitted with nickel steel armour plates mounted behind them. The aircraft proved to be very resistant to gun fire and often returned with 30 or more bullet holes. Until the end of the war 227 Junkers J Is were produced, of which 189 were delivered to front line units.

Before the end of the war, combat units were equipped with no more than 189 Junkers J I aircraft.

At the beginning of 1918, Schutzstaffeln (defensive squadrons) were renamed to Schlachtstaffeln (attack squadrons). The units were equipped with the Hannover CL II, CL III, CL IIIa, Halberstadt G.I and Junkers J I aircraft. Their basic task was to attack enemy infantry divisions approaching battlefields, artillery units and transport columns.

At the end of the war, during the allied attack in September 1918, 24 Halberstadt G.I attack aircraft managed to stop the whole British infantry division attacking the town of Péronne. One of the German pilots taking part in the mission remembers: "At 500 meters, after a signal given with a flare by our squadron commander, we formed two lines – one after another. In the destroyed Péronne, I saw only flames. The sparkling river band of Somme emerged from the smoke. After a few seconds, we were over the target – the troop columns. After another flare signal, we descended to 150 meters. We attacked with our machine guns coming down to 100 meters. After a turn, we re-engaged the target. Suddenly, from the left, two Sopwith 2F.1 fighters attacked us. We managed to shoot down one of them, the other one fled. We depleted all our ammunition in the second run then returned to our airfield, refueled, rearmed and repeated the attack. "[3]

In November of 1918, when the armistice was signed, Germany had 38 Schlachtstaffeln (attack squadrons) and two more were being created. The Treaty of Versailles ordered the Germans to hand over all their aviation equipment to the Allies and forbade further advancement of military aviation technology. It stopped the development of German close support aircraft for over ten years.

The concept of dive bombing appeared during World War I. After the national socialists had come to power in Germany on 30 January 1933, the restrictions imposed by the Treaty of Versailles were rejected. The quick reconstruction of the air force began. The trials of bombing in horizontal flight showed that, despite the participation of the most experienced crews, hitting the target spot on was just a matter of luck. The only method of precise target engagement was dive bombing. On 12 October 1933, Fliegergruppe Schwerin, the first dive bomber unit in the German air force was formed. The group flew the Heinkel He 50 aircraft.

The strong supporter of diver bombers was the Great War ace, Ernst Udet[4] who, on 27 September 1933, bought two F11C 2s in the Curtiss factory in Buffalo, USA. The aircraft were powered by the 712hp Wright SR-1820-F2 Cyclone engine that allowed the plane to reach speeds of 325 km/h at altitude of 1000 meters. Both aircraft were carefully packed in boxes and delivered to Germany on board the "Europa" passenger liner. In December 1933, the aircraft designated D-3165 and D-3166 (later changed to D-IRIS and D-ISIS) were transported to the experimental aviation research centre in Rechlin where Udet himself, presented the spectacular results of dive bombing. It turned out that dive bombers perfectly fit the new war doctrine. According to the concept called Blitzkrieg (lightning war), the German armed forces were to avoid long and destructive positional war during possible future conflict. Breaking through the front line swiftly and defeating the enemy in the manoeuvre war, was to be ensured by panzer units supported by the air force. Dive bombers were to be used as flying field artillery paving the way for panzer formations. The German air force development plan, announced in 1933, included so called Sofort-Programm (immediate program) to introduce a new type of dive bomber that would replace the Heinkel He 50 biplane. The new aircraft had to be a single seat machine with the ability to take 200kg bomb load. It was supposed to have the speed and

The all-metal Junkers CL I attack aircraft did not see combat during the Great War, the photograph shows the aircraft that served in the volunteer units operating in Latvia in 1919.

The American Curtiss Hawk II was the forerunner of German light dive bombers.

The first prototype of the Henschel Hs 123 V1 aircraft, D-ILUA on Berlin-Johannisthal airfield in May 1935.

manoeuvrability of a fighter, which would make the defensive armament redundant.

Two constructions entered the competition: Fieseler Fi 98 and Henschel Hs 123. The Fieseler Fi 98 was constructed by engineer Reinhold Mewes. It was a biplane of mixed structure, armed with two 7.92mm MG 17 machine guns and four bombs 50kg each. The power plant was the 650hp, BMW 132 A-3 radial engine. The aircraft's maximum speed was 295km/h, range was only 470km. The characteristic feature of

the plane was the twin elevator unit. The Fi 98 was test flown in spring of 1935 but did not meet the expectations of the competition committee. The Fieseler constructors built one more prototype designated Fi 98b and, with no success, tried to arouse the Japanese Navy's interest in their aircraft.

The Henschel Hs 123, produced by the Henschel Flugzeug Werke AG became the winner of the competition. The Henschel & Sohn AG works were created in 1848 as locomotive

HS 123 V1 during testing in the Luftwaffe experimental aviation research centre in Rechlin in September 1936.

factory and, at the end of the 19th century became the biggest European locomotive and rolling stock producer. When, in 1931, the Junkers Flugzeug und Motorwerke AG company in Dessau was in financial trouble, the Henschel & Sohn owners decided to broaden their production buying the Junkers works. The negotiations concerning the take-over of the Junkers company did not succeed and were sopped in the middle of February 1932. The negotiations to take over shares of other aviation companies met the same fate.

When the attempts to take control over one of German aviation companies, the chairman of the board of the Henschel & Sohn AG, Oscar R. Henschel authorized Walter Hormel, the president of the factory, to create an aviation department from scratch. During the meeting at the motor industry fair, on 11 February 1933, the Reich's Commissioner of Aerial Transport Hermann Göring (Reichskommissar für Luftverkehr) expressed his regrets when Oscar R. Henschel told him about difficulties with development of aviation production at his works. Göring promised to support Henschel in his further actions. A similar declaration was made by Erhard Milch, the Secretary of State in the Ministry of Aviation (Staatssekretär des Luftfahrtministeriums).

On 30 March 1933, near Kassel, the Henschel Flugzeug Werke GmbH was created with the capital of 500,000RM. Soon the works were turned into a stock company. Certified engineer Frydag became the technical president, CE Erich Koch was the chief constructor but was soon substituted by CE Friedrich Nicolaus.

On 17 May 1933, the Henschel aviation factory, located on the Berlin-Johannisthal airport, inaugurated its production. After seven months, on 4 January 1934, the first construction – the

The tail wheel of the Henschel Hs 123 V1 fitted with aerodynamic fairing.

Hs 121 single seat trainer – was test flown by prof. Scheubel. The Hs 121 was a monoplane with characteristic high-mounted gull wing (identical to that used by eng. Puławski from the Polish Państwowe Zakłady Lotnicze). The elliptic contour wings had two metal spars. Their front section was covered with metal sheets and other surfaces were covered with fabric. The front section of the oval shaped, metal structure fuselage, up to the cockpit was also covered with metal. The middle and tail sections were covered with fabric. Fabric was also used on all control surfaces and moving parts of the wings. The fixed undercarriage, covered by a metal fairing, had oil shock absorbers. The aircraft was powered by the Argus As 10C, 240hp, eight-cylinder inline engine. The construction turned out to be very unstable with poor reaction to controls.

Simultaneously, the Henschel works began licensed production of the Junkers W.33 and W.34. The production involved 142 white-collar workers and 570 labourers. The fast-growing company opened another factory in Berlin-Schönefeld on 22 December 1935. It was a huge plant built after 10,000 train transports had delivered all necessary materials. It had the

Additional armament, the So 1-FMP-Anlage system with two machine pistols mounted in the top wing did not prove itself so it was not featured in production aircraft.

Hs 122 A-0 and on the very next day, the first Dornier Do 23 (Wn. 254) – one of 24 aircraft built under licence. The Henschel Hs 122 did not meet the requirements of the Reich's Ministry of Aviation (RLM – Reichsluftfahrtministerium) and only 19 aircraft were produced. The first machine built in large quantities by the Berlin-Schönefeld works was the Henschel 123. The first three aircraft left the factory in 1936. During the World War II, the Henschel company produced large numbers of their own constructions like Hs 123, Hs 126 and Hs 129 but also Dornier Do 17 and Junkers Ju 188 under licence.

The construction department of the company was also involved in many innovative and technologically advanced projects of remotely controlled bombs (Hs 293, Hs 294, Hs 295, Hs 196 and Hs 297), anti aircraft missiles (Hs 117 and Hs 217) and air-to-air missiles (Hs 298). In 1944, during its best period, the Henschel Fluzeug Werke AG owned eight huge production plants and employed 67,000 workers, including 17,100 in the aviation production.

whole system of railway sidings and its own power plant with capacity to provide electricity for a town with 40,000 inhabitants.

On 2 January 1936, the new factory saw the test flight of the reconnaissance Henschel

The Henschel Hs 123's rival was the Fieseler Fi 98 with unusual elevator unit structure.

Henschel 123 V2, W.Nr 0266 with the Wright Cyclone GR-1820-F52, 770hp engine.

Prototypes

Hs 123 V1

Work on the first prototype of the Henschel Hs 123 V1 was inaugurated in February 1934. The initial concept saw the aircraft as a light dive bomber capable of performing fighter tasks. In June 1934, a full scale wooden model was built and the first prototype was constructed on 1 April 1935. A few days later, on the Berlin-Schönefeld airport, the first test flights began. The aircraft with the production number Wn. 0265, painted entirely in RLM 01 Grau, was given civilian designation D-ILUA. The machine did not have any armament and was powered by the BMW 132A, air-cooled, 9-cylinder, radial engine. It was a licenced version of the American Pratt & Whitney Hornet with maximum power of 725hp at 2,050rpm. The Hs 123 V1 was introduced to the Luftwaffe representatives on 8 May 1935 on the Berlin-Johannisthal airport. Among the Luftwaffe representatives was Ernst Udet, who did not resist the temptation to sit at the controls of the new aircraft. During the test flight, Udet performed several dives.

On 2 June 1935, the aircraft was transferred to the experimental center in Rechlin where it was tested from the end of June 1935 until January of the following year. On 4 February 1936, the tests of the So I-17 installation were concluded. The installation comprised two 7.92mm MG 17 machine guns mounted on the upper part of the engine cowling and a synchronizer allowing for firing through the propeller. Each gun had 500 rounds of ammunition. A different set up was also tested, the So 1-FMP installation included two machine pistols with 100 rounds per gun, mounted on the upper wing. The configuration was very ineffective so the idea was dropped.

Until May 1936, the Henschel Hs 123 V1 had 95.8 flight hours. In May 1936, further 49 flights (total of 5 hours 56 minutes) were performed. The tests concerned brakes of the main undercarriage and tires of the 290x110mm tail wheel fitted with aerodynamic fairing.

The aircraft remained in Rechlin until September 1936 and then, after mounting the radial BMW 132 A engine, transferred to a Luftwaffe unit.

Hs 123 V2

In the middle of May 1935 another prototype of the Henschel Hs 123 V2, Wn. 0266 was built. Its factory tests were inaugurated on 15 June 1935. One of the first to fly the machine was the Reich's Ministry of Aviation inspector for single seat aircraft, Major Robert Ritter von Greim.[5] The prototype was also tested by von

Greim's adjutant, the later Stuka ace, Hptm. Oscar Dinort.[6]

The Hs 123 V2 did not have civilian registration. Its power plant was the American, nine-cylinder, radial Wright Cyclone GR-1820-F52 engine with the maximum power of 770hp at 2150rpm. The engine had a smooth NACA type cowling. The use of the foreign power plant was not accepted by the Reich's Ministry of Aviation and the project was rejected.

From the beginning of 1936, the aircraft was tested in the Rechlin experimental centre where, among others, strength tests of the ailerons were conducted. After the tests had been completed, the Technical Department of the RLM ordered the installation of two 7.92mm MG 17 machine guns on the Hs 123 V2.

In autumn of 1936, while landing on the Berlin-Schönefeld factory airport, the aircraft nosed-over and was seriously damaged. The pilot was unharmed. The accident created an opportunity to replace the American Wright Cyclone with the German BMW 132 A-3 engine. After being refitted with the new engine, with all damage repaired in spring of 1937, the aircraft was designated Hs 123 V8.

Hs 123 V2 with characteristic smooth NACA type engine cowling.

The third Hs 123 V3 prototype, D-IKOU with three-colour national markings on the vertical stabilizer.

Hs 123 V3

The third prototype, the Henschel Hs 123 V3, Wn. 0267, D-IKOU was built in May 1935 and test flown a month later. Until the end of May 1936, the aircraft had 77.8 hours of flying time. The testing included a new elastic fuel tank and the So 1 II-Würfe system used for bomb release from underneath the lower wings. The aiming device was the Revi IIIb reflex sight.[7] The armament tests were conducted by Oberst Ernst Udet himself. What followed, were 28 take offs with the Kronprinz 290x110mm tail wheel. During one of the landings, in June 1936, the aircraft was severely damaged. The slightly damaged airframe was repaired in in the workshops of the Rechlin research centre but the wings were sent to the Henschel factory in Berlin-Schönefeld.

In August 1936, after the repairs had been completed, the aircraft was subjected to another month of testing in Rechlin. After all trials, it was decided that the aircraft would remain in the research centre. On 1 April 1937 it was completely destroyed in a crash. When pulling from a dive, the strut connecting the upper wing with the fuselage broke causing the entire wing to break off. The pilot, Heinz Wulf from the Fieseler Flugzeugbau GmbH died in the crash.

Hs 123 V4

Before the early prototypes were test flown, in March 1935, the RLM had requested the Henschel company to prepare equipment allowing for quick commencement of the Hs 123 serial production. The standard aircraft for the pre-production machines designated Hs 123 A-0

The same Hs 123 V3 aircraft with the national markings repainted on the vertical stabilizers.

Hs 123 V3, D-IKOU with four SC 50 bombs under the wings.

was to be the fourth prototype, The Hs 123 V4, Wn. 0670, D-IZXY powered by the BMW 132 A engine. The assembly of the fourth prototype was delayed for four and a half months and the aircraft was not ready for take off until the middle of April 1936.

Within the next month, the machine was test flown on the Schönefeld airport. The testing continued from September to November 1936 in Rechlin where the aircraft was fitted with the So II installation consisting of ten Elvemag 5C 10 bomb containers mounted vertically in the fuselage. Each container held one S.C. 10, 10kg fragmentation bomb. However, the test results were not satisfactory for the representatives of the Technical Department of the Reich's Ministry of Aviation. Access to the containers on the ground and mounting bombs were very difficult. What was more, the effectiveness of 10kg bombs dropped on targets from horizontal flight was far from being satisfactory. Finally, it was decided to fit the production Hs 123s with the So III bomb installation allowing for mounting two 50kg bombs under the lower wing.

The fourth prototype, Hs 123 V4, D-IZXY.

Henschel 123 V5, D-INRA with the BMW 132 J engine and the Junkers-Hamilton adjustable pitch propeller.

After the Rechlin tests, the Hs 123 V4 was transferred to one of the Luftwaffe units. When the Hs 123 V3 crashed on 1 April 1937, the Hs 123 V4 was sent to the Henschel works where the struts were replaced and their attachment points with the fuselage and the upper wing strengthened.

Hs 123 V5

The Henschel Hs 123 V5 was the 16th Hs 123 A-1 production aircraft. It was to be fitted with the Junkers Jumo 210 C, 610hp inline engine. Before the aircraft assembly was completed, a change of the power plant was suggested in

Hs 123 V5 participated in the "4th International Aviation Meeting" on the Dübendorf airfield in Switzerland in 1937. It came second in the flight speed competition, just behind the BF 109 fighter.

Henschel 123 V7, D-IHBO.

favour of the 800hp, BMW 132F radial engine. At the end of June 1936, the RLM made another decision, the Hs 123 V5, Wn. 0769, D-INRA was to be given the latest BMW 132G engine with 830hp at 2230rpm. However, before the engine had been mounted, even more powerful power plant appeared. The BMW 132J had the power of 910hp at 2250rpm. The RLM changed their decision again and, in January 1937, the Hs 123 V5 was equipped with the BMW 132J engine. The new power plant required a larger oil radiator and cowling. The aircraft was given the Junkers-Hamilton three-blade, metal propeller with adjustable pitch and a 50cm diameter spinner. The idea to use a closed canopy did not come into fruition.

Since the aircraft was to be shown during the 4th International Aviation Meeting on the Dübendorf airport in Switzerland, the Hs 123 V5 assembly was concluded at the end of May 1937. On 28 May 1937, during the meeting of the representatives of the Henschel works in Berlin-Schönefeld with CE Frank from the research centre command, a decision was made to send the aircraft on 20 July 1937 to the meeting in Switzerland. CE Othmar Schürfeld, one of the Rechlin experimental centre test pilots, was chosen to fly the aircraft.

34 machines from different countries took part in the meeting. Germany, apart from the Hs 123 V5, presented six pre-production Messerschmitt Bf 109 aircraft and the Dornier Do 17

Henschel 123 A-1 in the production hall, details of the BMW 132 A-3 engine are clearly visible.

Henschel 123 A-1 on the Henschel Flugzeugwerke AG factory airfield. Under the fuselage, additional 130 litre fuel tank can be seen.

V8 bomber. One of the events was to ascend to 3000 meters and dive towards the finish line on the ground. The winner was Carl Franke, with the result of 2 minutes and 23 seconds, piloting the Messerschmitt Bf 109 V7, D-IJHA powered by the Junkers Jumo 210G, 730hp engine. The second place was taken by Othmar Schürfeld in the Henschel Hs 123 V5, who was only 17.3 seconds slower than Franke.

In August 1937, the RLM decided to fit the Hs 123 V5 with the BMW 132K V 109 engine. The new engine, serial number 55053, arrived at the Henschel factory, with a one month delay, in October 1937. The BMW 132K with the power of 960hp at 2550rpm was another de-

velopment of the BMW 132F equipped with additional injection of methyl alcohol mixture. The BMW 132K used the C2 type fuel. Mounting of the new power plant in the Hs 123 V5 prolonged until the beginning of January 1938. Then, the aircraft was transferred to Rechlin, where within the following month numerous tests were conducted. The results were satisfactory and, in February 1938, the aircraft returned to the Berlin works and later was to be transferred to the Luftwaffe unit. However, in March 1938, a serious malfunction of the power plant forced the replacement of the engine. Fitted with new engine, the machine was sent to Rechlin in May 1938 and later, on 12 January 1939,

Henschel Hs 123 A-1 with civilian designation D-IKSW.

Henschel Hs 123 A-1 being prepared for the 1937 Berlin exhibition.

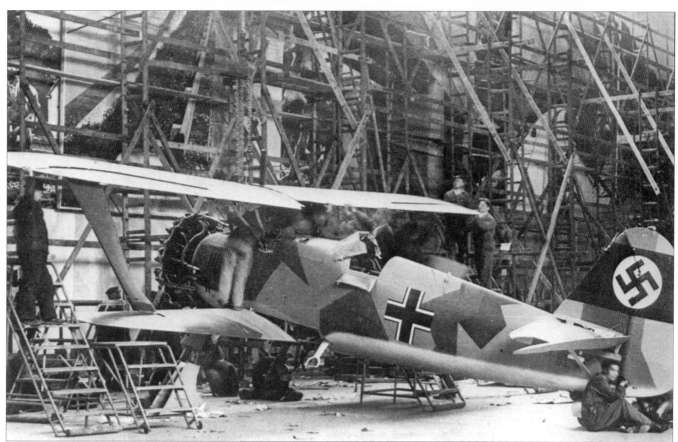

Hs 123 A-1 from I./St.G 165 on the Kitzingen airfield in 1937.

The Henschel Hs 123 A-1 aircraft serving in St.G 162.

Henschel Hs 123 A-1 from 3./St.G 165.

The Henschel Hs 123 A-1 aircraft from 3./St.G 165 during a training flight. The photograph includes machines designated 52+A13, 52+D13 and 52+H13.

after another series of tests, the aircraft finally entered the Luftwaffe service.

Hs 123 V6

The Henschel Hs 123 V6, Wn. 0797 was the 17th A-1 version production aircraft and, like the Hs123 V5, was initially to be powered by the inline Junkers Jumo 210C engine and later by the radial BMW 132F. Finally, the airframe was to be fitted with the BMW 132K with additional injection of methyl alcohol mixture. Due to slow progress of the engine development, the

Hs 123 A-1 during the 1937 Luftwaffe equipment exhibition.

RLM ordered the Henschel factory to introduce changes into the aileron construction. Finally, in May 1937, the BMW 132J was delivered and mounted on the Hs 123 V6 prototype along with the three-blade, adjustable pitch VDM propeller.

The aircraft was designated D-IHDI and, on 20 June 1937, flew to Friedrichshafen as a reserve machine for the Hs 123 V5 taking part in the meeting in Switzerland. From 6 August 1937, the aircraft was on the BMW factory airfield in München-Allach where its power plant was tested. In summer of 1938, the plane

was transferred to Rechlin where it was fitted with a closed canopy. The aircraft was tested in diving and numerous bomb drops were conducted. During testing, the fuselage fuel tank was enlarged and a bomb of up to 500kg was mounted in place of the drop tank. The testing included the So III installation that allowed for carrying eight 50kg or four 50kg bombs under the wings and a 250kg one under the fuselage. There were also tests of two fixed MG 17, 7.92 machine guns with 500 rounds of ammunition each, mounted on the lower wing. The aircraft with the BMW 132J engine, closed canopy and additional MG 17 machine guns was the prototype of a planned Hs 123 C version.

Hs 132 V7

In November 1936, the RLM ordered the Henschel factory to produce the seventh prototype, the Hs 132 V7 that was to be used for testing with the new BMW 132 K engine with a three-blade propeller.

The Hs 132 V7 was the A-1 version production airframe with serial number Wn. 0985. The aircraft had enlarged fuel tank which allowed for mounting a 250kg bomb in place of the 130dm³ drop tank.

Because of the slow progress of the power plant testing and increasing amount of work on other Henschel company designs (Hs 124 and Hs 127 fast bombers), the assembly of the Hs 123 V7 was not completed until late autumn of 1937. On 26 October 1937, the Bayerische Motoren Werke delivered the BMW 132 J engine to the Henschel factory in Berlin-Schönefeld. The prototype received civilian designation D-IHBO and had its maiden flight in November 1937. The target engine, BMW 132 K V 110, serial number 55054, was not delivered until June 1938. When it was mounted in the Hs 123 V7 in the second half of June 1938, the aircraft was sent to the Rechlin research centre. The majority of the test flights was conducted by test pilot Reck from the E3 department. On 5 September 1938 the testing was concluded and the aircraft was taken over by the Luftwaffe.

Hs 123 V8

After the crash of the Hs 123 V2 fitted with the American Wright Cyclone GR-1820-F 52 engine, the RLM made a decision to repair the aircraft which after mounting the BMW 132A-3 was to be a standard aircraft for the A-1 version. The machine was designated D-IUPO. The total cost of repairs and rebuilding the plane, was 12,458RM. In August 1937 the aircraft entered service in the Luftwaffe and was handed over to the Office of Aviation Equipment (Luftzeugamt) in Kölleda.

Production aircraft

Hs 123 A-0

In March 1935 the Henschel works began preparations for production of the A-0 version of the Henschel Hs 123 which was to be based on the Hs 123 V4 airframe. On 22 June 1935, a contract for the aircraft delivery was signed between the RLM and the Henschel company. Between July 1936 and January 1937, the Berlin-Schönefeld factory produced 16 Henschel Hs 123 A-0s with serial numbers from Wn. 0628 to 0635 and from 0788 to 0795. In August 1937, by the order of the Reich's Ministry of Aviation, the aircraft was tested in the Luftwaffe units. The testing was concluded in December 1937.

Hs 123 A and Hs 123 B

The serial production of the Henschel 123 A-1 began in January 1936, the first aircraft were built in September of the same year. Due to mounting problems with material, only six Hs 123 A-1 aircraft were produced until 30 November 1936. The production gained momentum in

Another view of the 3./St.G Hs 123 A-1 formation.

Three Hs 123 A-1s from St.G 165: W.Nr. 0968, 52+A13, W.Nr. 0969, 52+B13 and W.Nr. 0970, 52+C13.

Henschel Hs 123 A-1, W.Nr. 0968, 52+A13 from 2./St.G 165 in 1937.

Hs 123 A-1 with the undercarriage leg broken during a hard landing.

in 1937 and was used for testing the metal skin for ailerons that was later used in the B-1 version aircraft.

Hs 123 C

The prototype of the C version was the Hs 123 V6 with the BMW 132 J engine, closed canopy and two additional MG 17 machine guns mounted under the lower wings with 500 rounds of ammunition per gun. However, the C version did not enter serial production.

Pre-war period

After its rebirth on 1 March 1935, the German air force began rapid development. One of the main tasks of the Luftwaffe command was to create units equipped with dive bombers and attack aircraft that could support ground forces on the battlefield. Two kinds of such units were created, regiments of dive bombers (Stukageschwader, St.G) and squadrons of attack aircraft (Schlachtfliegergruppen, SFGr.). After the commencement of the Henschel 123 serial production, the first aircraft were deployed to I./St.G 162 stationed at the Schwerin airfield, at the end of 1936. The squadron was formerly equipped with the Heinkel He 50 and Arado Ar 65 aircraft. Then, the new machines were delivered to SFGr. 10 and SFGr. 50. The Henschel Hs 123 was also the first aircraft of the newly formed dive bomber squadrons – III./St.G 165, I./St.G 163, II./St.G 162, I./St.G 167 and St.G 168. After another reorganization in summer of 1938 when the attack units were changed into dive bomber units, the Henschel Hs 123 aircraft remained only in SFGr. 10 stationed on the Tutow airfield in Mecklenburg-Vorpommern. In November 1938 the squadron became part of Lehrgeschwader 2 and was renamed to II.(Schl.)/LG 2.

December 1936 when further 15 machines left the factory.

From August 1936 to April 1937, the Henschel Hs A-1 aircraft were also produced under licence in the AGO Flugzeugwerke GmbH in Oschersleben. In 1937, a small number of the Hs 123 B-1s was produced. The aircraft had their ailerons and larger part of the wing surface covered with metal instead of fabric. The total of 265 Hs 123 aircraft were produced including 129 in the AGO factory.

Apart from seven prototypes, several production Hs 123s were used for different tests. One of them was the Wn. 0788 with the BMW 132 J V 55 (serial number 55042) engine. The same engine was mounted on the Hs 123 Wn. 0789. Two other aircraft with serial numbers Wn. 0819 and 2247 served as dive bombers in the Rechlin experimental centre. The Hs 123 A-1, Wn. 0958 remained in the Henschel works

Legion Condor

In the second week of September 1936, the Reich's government decided to support General Franco's troops fighting against the communist government of Spain. The operation was given the codename "Feuerzauber". The first two Henschel Hs 123 A-0s were packed in boxes and, in September 1936, shipped aboard the German freighter "Wigbert" to the port of Cadiz. The aircraft were assembled and test flown on the Tablada airfield near Seville. In October 1936, the third Hs 123 A-0 was delivered and a flight of dive bombers (Patrulla de bombardeo en picado) was formed. Initially it was stationed on the Jarez de la Frontera airfield. From

December 1936, the flight was placed under the command of the Versuchs Jagdgruppe 88 (VJ/88), the 88 experimental fighter squadron of the Legion Condor. The first three Hs 123 A-0s delivered to Spain had fuselage markings 24•1, 24•2 i 24•3. Leutnant Heinrich Brücker, called "Rubio" (the Blonde) by his Spanish colleagues, became the commander of the dive bombers flight. The other two aircraft were flown by Uffz. Emil Rückert i Uffz. August Wilmsen.

On 25 March 1937, the flight suffered its first casualty. The aircraft piloted by Uffz. Rückert was hit by anti aircraft artillery over Aravaca – one of the suburban towns near Madrid. The German pilot bailed out over the front line but, during his descent, was fired at by enemy infantry and was seriously wounded.

The event was observed by a Moroccan soldier Aomar Ben Abdelá from 6 Company of Grupo de Fuerzas Regulares Indigenas No. 4 „Larache". Accompanied by his friends, he rushed to help the German pilot who landed on no man's land, near the wreckage of his aircraft. When they reached the crashed machine, they used it as cover against the enemy machine gun fire. The Franquista soldiers managed to find the pilot who had already died of his wounds.

At the end of March 1937, another three Hs 123 As were delivered to Spain. They were designated 24•4, 24•5 and 24•6. Along with the new equipment, two pilots – Fw. Fritz Hillmann and Uffz. Hermann Beurer were assigned to VJ/88.

On 1 April 1936, VJ/88 was dissolved and the Hs 123 As were attached to an independent squadron, Stuka/88. The personnel of the new unit consisted of 15 people including two civilians – Werner Busch and Walter Krone from The Henschel company. The squadron's emblem painted on the side of the aircraft's fuselage, in front of the cockpit, was the red devil's head.

Stuka/88 was soon transferred from near Madrid to the Vitoria airfield. The unit participated in the final phase of the battle of Bilbao. During the siege of Bilbao, the republican anti aircraft artillery shot down the second Hs 123 A over Ochandiano on 22 May 1937. Its pilot

Hs 123 A-1 from St.G 165 taking off for a training flight.

Hs 123 A-1, W.Nr. 0831, 52+A12 from 2./St.G 165 damaged in emergency landing during the summer manoeuvres in 1937.

Flight of Hs 123 A-1s from 3./ St.G 165 during the Anchluß of Austria on 12 March 1938.

was unharmed. The third Hs 123 was shot down on 11 June 1937 near Cinturón de Hierro during the attack on field fortifications. This time, the pilot – Uffz. August Wilmsen – did not survive the crash.

In August 1937, both surviving Henschel 123s were donated to the Spanish air force.

Polish campaign

On 1 August 1939, II.(Schl.)/LG 2 was transferred from the Tutow airfield to Altsiedel in Silesia. The squadron had 40 aircraft, 36 of which were ready for action. The commanding officer was Maj. Werner Spielvogel.

II.(Schl.)/LG 2 was part of the Luftflote 4 (4th Air Fleet) commanded by Gen.d.Fl. Alexander Löhr. The unit was operationally subordinated to to the Fliegerführer z.b.V (special deployment air force commander) commanded by Gen. Maj. dr eng. Wolfram Freiherr von Richthofen.

Wolfram Freiherr von Richthofen, whose cousin was the most famous World War I fighter ace, initially served as a hussar. After the death of his famous cousin, he became the member of Jagdstaffel 11 at the beginning of April 1918 and until the end of the war scored 8 aerial victories. After the war he finished his studies and in 1923 joined the Reichswehr. In 1929 he became the military attache in Rome and in 1933 joined the air force. In November 1939 he

became the Legion Condor commander's (Gen. Maj. Hugo Sperrle) chief of staff. He was promoted two years later to Generalmajor. At the same time he was given the command of the Legion Condor. After the war in Spain, he became the commanding officer of the special air force and then the commander of VIII. Fliegerkorps (VIII Air Corps).

Von Richthofen had already learned about the weak spots of the Henschel Hs 123 during the war in Spain. Because of the aircraft's short operational range, he ordered the unit to be redeployed from Altsiedel to Alt-Rosenberg, close to the Polish border.[8]

The morning of 1 September 1939, in II.(Schl.)/LG 2's area of operations, was moist and foggy. Gen.Maj. Wolfram Freiherr von Richthofen at his command centre started to receive reports of the first losses among his units. Just before dawn, one of the first aircraft to cross the Polish border were the Henschel 123s. The events that unfolded were colorfully described by Cajus Bekker: "On the Luftflotte 4's direction of operations, the atmospheric conditions are better but the weather is not perfect for flying. It is still dark when Generalmajor von Richthofen crosses the short distance from the Schönwald palace to the border.. The watch shows a few minutes after half past five. In less than a quarter the whole border will become the front line. The air corpse commander's Kübelwagen is moving, with its headlights blacked-out, along the endless columns of infantry. Finally, it stops in the area of the labour camp. From here, Richthofen has to walk about a kilometre to his command post, south of the Grunsruh border crossing. He is accompanied by his orderly, Oberleutnant Beckhaus.

Half way through, they heard the rattling of the infantry's gunfire. Further north, the artillery salvos thundered.

'It is exactly 4.45, Sir!' Beckhaus reported. Richthofen nodded. He stood in one place listening to the sounds of the night.

The Hs 123 A-1 aircraft of dive bomber units were replaced by the Junkers Ju 87 Stuka. In the photograph, aircraft from I./St.G 162 on the Schwerin airfield.

Henschel Hs 123 A-1,
WL+IPNC from the Sch./FAR
41 aviation school, Frankfurt/
Oder, September 1939.

'The first shots made me feel strange' – he later wrote in his personal diary – "Now the situation will be serious. Until now, I have thought only about strictly political solutions or the 'flower war'[9]. I am thinking of France and Britain and somehow I do not believe in a political solution of the conflict that has just begun. The fifteen-minute-long walk to the command center was marked with serious concern for the future. However, when Seidemann gave me his report in the command post, all worries disappeared. What was important, was the material approach towards the war that had broken out...'

The sun was beginning ti rise. It was moist. Clouds of fog hugged the ground. 'Not very fly-able weather' – said the chief of staff, Oberst-leutnant Hans Seidemann – 'When the sun goes up, the Sukas will not be able to see the ground through the fog.'

First reports of the aircraft taking off, reach the command post. Richthofen goes outside. It is still unusually quiet. There are no sounds of fighting. Just single shots. There are not many signs of the ongoing war. After a while, shortly before the sunrise, our attack aircraft approach. They come closer. The attack squadron II.(Schl.)/LG 2 commanded by Major Spielvogel took off according to schedule from the Altsiedel air-field. The Henschel 123s fly in circles over the border river buzzing like angry hornets.

They look a little outdated: strange bi-planes with thick, round radial engine and the pilot sitting unprotected in the open cockpit. Nothing is anonymous here, nothing can be hidden. No cockpit armour, no glass canopies. The strike aircraft, as they are called, are pi-loted by full breed pilots, the old school, face to face with the enemy.

Hptm. Otto Weiß, the commander of 1. Staffel II. (Schl.)/LG 2, saw the target on the other side – the village of Panki (Przystajn) where the Poles had dug in.[10] Weiß raised his hand to show the target to his companions and pointed his aircraft downwards for attack. Now, even here in the south directly in front of the 10. Army the first bombs fall: the light "Flambos" (incendiary bombs) with impact fuse. They explode with a thud on the ground, burn-ing everything around, covering the area with smoke and flames. The course of the raid can be seen from the command post of the spe-cial deployment air force. The second attack squadron is led by Oblt. Adolf Galland, later the famous fighter ace. The remaining squadrons jump over the tree tops firing their guns at the Polish positions.

Meanwhile, the muffled fire of the light anti aircraft artillery can be heard. The enemy is be-ginning to defend himself. The infantry weapons can also be heard. The firing escalates and con-tinues long after the strike planes fly away."[11]

Four aircraft did not return from the first combat mission to the Altsiedel airfield. Fortu-

Hs 123 A-1, CH+?W, white 5
from one of the training units.

The first Hs 123 A-1 sent to Spain as a test aircraft of VJ/88, Tablada airfield.

netely, three of them were soon found and their pilots Lt.d.Res. Wöhrl, Fw. Zeltner and Oblt. Egon Thiem returned to their unit before noon. Uffz. Arthur Kracht was shot down near Kłobuck by the Polish anti aircraft artillery and was taken prisoner. Kracht, from Thüringen (Thuringia) was 22 when soldiers from the Polish 15 Infantry Regiment captured him. During interrogation he testified that he had been sent to Cottbus to fetch an aircraft to the Sagan airfield but, due to difficult weather conditions, got lost and crashed his machine 8km north east of Wieluń.

The operation at Krzepice/Panki was the first close air support mission conducted by the Luftwaffe attack aircraft in the World War II.

Between 11.45 and 13.30, thirty Henschel 123 As attacked and armoured train and railway targets near the Popów station.

In the afternoon, II.(Schl.)/LG 2 flew another two combat missions, 30 aircraft each. The first one, from 14.35 to 15.30 and the second between 16.30 and 17.36. During the second mission, Fw. Neszerie crash landed near the town of Noldau.

On the first day of the war, the attack squadron dropped 519 SC 50, two SD 50, 586 SC 10 bombs and 38 containers with incendiary bombs.[12]

On Saturday, 2 September 1939 at 09.30, several reserve Henschel Hs 123 A aircraft for II.(Schl.)/LG 2 arrived at the Alt-Rosenberg airfield. At that time 18 aircraft of 5. and 6. Staffel were conducting a combat mission. Betwee 11.09 and 12.16, machines from 5. and 6. Staffel took off again, this time supported by the staff flight. At 12.20, the aircraft of 4. Staffel took

off from Altsiedel accompanied by the staff machines. After completing their mission, all aircraft safely landed in Alt-Rosenberg at 13.55. Between 15.00 and 15.40 another combat mission was conducted by the aircraft of the staff/HQ flight and 6. Staffel. The last combat action of the day was flown, between 15.08 and 16.06 by the pilots from 4. and 5. Staffel. At 17.15 all aircraft of II.(Schl.)/LG 2 flew from Alt-Rosenberg to Altsiedel.

At 09.45, on Sunday 3 September 1939, 17 Hs 123 As from 4. and 5.(Schl.)/LG 2 took off from the Altsiedel airfield. Their task was to attack military transport columns at the rear of the front line. They were to be escorted by the Messerschmitt Bf 109s from 3./ZG 2 which, however, failed to show up at the rendezvous point. Near Piotrków, the unprotected Henschels were engaged by four Polish PZL P.11c fighters from 161 Fighter Squadron. A short dogfight ensued, one of the Polish fighters was shot down, the others fled. The Germans did not suffer any losses. During the return flight to the home airfield, the machine piloted by Lt. Panten got lost. The Henschel landed, at 11.45, at the Kreuzberg airfield and after refueling returned to Alt-Rosenberg where it crashed during landing and was damaged in 40%. The other aircraft landed safely at 11.16.

The pilots from II.(Schl.)/LG 2 did not fly combat missions until Tuesday 5 September 1939 when the squadron aircraft were transferred to the Witkowice airfield, 16 kilometres north west of Częstochowa. The Hs 123s landed there between 09.30 and 10.00. At 10.45, four machines from 4. Staffel took off for the first combat mission from their new airfield and returned at 11.24. At 12.15, eight Hs 123s from 6. Staffel took off to bomb the train station in Opoczno. Between 14.36 and 15.15, nine Hs 123s from 5. Staffel attacked Polish units 4 kilometres east of Piotrków. The same target was later bombed by another four Henschels from 5. Staffel (take off at 15.35) and then by twelve machines from 4. Staffel (take off at 15.47, landing at 16.32). In the area of Piotrków there were also aircraft from 6. Staffel (three machines took off at 16.32). The last mission of the day was flown between 17.00 and 17.50 by seventeen Hs 123 aircraft from Stab, 5. and 6. Staffel.

On Wednesday, 6 September 1939, the pilots of II.(Schl.)/LG 2 started their combat actions between 08.27 and 09.22 when the aircraft from 5. and 6. Staffel took off to destroy Polish group formations hidden in the forest north east of Piotrków and Koło. They did not find their targets in the indicated area, so the twenty Hs 123s bombed the train station in Tomaszów Mazowiecki.

Another three actions (between 12.00 and 14.00) were conducted by the pilots of 4. Staffel who, in the force of a Schwarm, attacked the cavalry, anti tank artillery positions and vehicles in the forest west of Tomaszów Mazowiecki. In the afternoon (between 16.10 and 17.15) another twelve Hs 123s from Stab and 5. Staffel participated in the raids. At 17.37, nine more Hs 123s of 4. Staffel took off and flew in the direction of Tomaszów, where, at the train station, two freight trains ready to depart were attacked and immobilized. The Henschels dropped their

remaining bombs on a large military column moving along the Tomaszów-Lubochnia road.

During the first days of the war, the aircraft of II.(Schl.)/LG 2 accompanied the troops of the XVI. Army Corps in their march on Warsaw. Wherever the soldiers encountered strong opposition, the attack aircraft appeared. The results of their raids far exceeded the combat potential of those light machines. The mystery was solved when it turned out that propellers driven by the BMW 132 A engine working at high revolutions (above 1,800rpm), made a sound closely resembling the heavy sound of a large caliber machine gun. The sight of a biplane flying 10 metres above the ground with a clatter of machine guns, scared horses and caused panic among enemy soldiers. Interesting is the

Hs 123 A-1, 24●5, flown by Lt. Hein Brückner, the fuselage is marked with the unit's emblem, the devil's head.

The Stukakette/88 emblem painted on the Hs 123 aircraft in Spain.

fact that at such high revolutions of the engine, the machine gun synchronizer would not work and pilots could not open fire in order not to damage the propeller blades. The psychological effect of such attacks was given a special name" akustische Kopfwelle"[13], it was particularly effective during attacks against marching columns, almost every time scaring horses that were the main transportation means for artillery and materiel.

During the attack of eight Hs 123 As from 6. Staffel on a military column near Sławno in the afternoon of 7 September 1939, the Polish anti aircraft artillery shot down the Hs 123 A piloted by the flight commander, Oblt. Friedrich Lampe. The burned wreckage of the aircraft and the pilot's body were found by the Flugmeldekompanie in the field between Sławno

A pair of the Hs 123 A-1 aircraft, in the foreground 24●2, in the background 24●3.

Hs 123 A-1, 24●3 shortly after arriving in Spain, the early production aircraft.

Henschel Hs 123 A-1, 24●3 on the Alfaro airfield in 1938.

Hs 123 A-1, 24•5 on an airstrip.

Interesting view of the Hs 123 A-1 without the main undercarriage fairings.

and Radonie, west of Opoczno. The pilot was buried near the crash site.

During the combat mission conducted by nine Hs 123s of 4. Staffel, between 14.35 and 15.30, a military column withdrawing along the road near Opoczno was bombed. Later, from 16.00 and 17.15, nine Hs 123s from 5. Staffel operated in the same area. One of the Henschels emergency landed on friendly territory, damaging the lower wing, undercarriage and the oil pipe. Between 07.32 and 07.50 on 8 September 1939, the Hs 123 As of II.(Schl.)/LG 2 flew to the airfield, near Tomaszów. The runway was the stubble near the Wolbórz stables. The field was chosen according to the rule practised by the attack pilots: "If we were able to drive through a field in a car packed with 50 different things and the whole stuff did not make much noise, that meant the field was good enough for our Hs 123s to take off and land".[14] The task was not very difficult as the Hs 123 needed only 200 metres of the runway. After the death of Oblt. Lampe, the command of 6. Staffel was taken by Oblt. Peitsmeyer.

Two Hs 123 A-1 of the later production series, in the background, 24•12 aircraft can be seen.

Hs 123 A-1, 24●5, on the side of the forward part of the fuselage, the unit's emblem, the devil's head can be seen.

Gen.Maj. Dr.Ing. Wolfram Freiherr von Richthofen, during the September campaign of 1939 the commanding officer of Fliegerführer z.b.V. (special deployment air force command).

The squadron began its operations from the new airfield at 09.06 (take off of 5. Staffel). During the day, the aircraft carried out at least ten big missions against columns of Polish troops withdrawing towards Warsaw. After a few combat missions it turned out the squadron was running out of bombs so it could not operate in full strength. In the early afternoon, the advanced units of the 4. Panzer Division accompanied from the air by the Hs 123s of II.(Schl.)/ LG 2 reached the suburbs of Warsaw. One of the squadrons operations was presented by war correspondent Curt Strohmeyer:

"It is wonderful cloudless afternoon. We are lying on the ground, looking at the sky, so we are doing what every airman does willingly to let his strained senses relax. It is not that easy as the amount of emotions from previous days affected us all. The feeling of inevitable victory here in Poland has been strong for some time now. It is related to the trust we put in our weapons that fall like lightnings from the sky so there can be nothing more beautiful than the order: 'Combat mission!' Meanwhile, nothing is happening. We are having a nap in the warm sun. Somebody tells a stupid joke, someone else is sitting against a bush, playing the harmonica.

Its sound is mixed with the far noise of an aircraft engine. We can hear it perfectly and immediately recognize one of our planes. We presume it is a reconnaissance machine of the ground forces. Our heated senses get sharper as the aircraft gets closer. We see it and it seems the pilot is looking for us, so we get up and start waving at him. After a while he is circling over our airfield. Suddenly, he changes his course and flies directly towards the command post. We see a bag with a report fall from the aircraft and land almost exactly at the command post. The paper reads:'Large column marching from west towards Warsaw. Raid with high probability of success. Follow me!'.

At the same time our flight is ready for take off. The engines are singing their inspiring song. The machines taxi on the ground, take off, the flight gets into formation and when we are following the reconnaissance aircraft we see the rest of the squadron getting ready for take off. The weather is wonderful. Great for flying.

The Henschel Hs 123 A-1 aircraft from II.(Schl.)/LG 2 in flight over Poland, in the foreground L2+BM aircraft piloted by Adolf Galland who later become a fighter ace.

There is a delicate mist below but it does not obscure our view. The sun reflects in the matt paint masking our aircraft and we, eagerly waiting for the oncoming fight, are contemplating the the flight itself.

The commander first spotted the trail of the enemy. Below, on the road leading from the west to Warsaw, there is a huge military column on the move. It is so big, it is divided into three parallel ones, marching or riding alongside at a long distance. They are certainly units pushed out from the area of Kutno, now marching as fast as possible to Warsaw to regroup and prepare to counter attack. When we get closer, we see every branch of the armed forces, there is infantry, motorized units, artillery, ammunition trucks, anti tank cannons and endless supply wagons. The commander had already reported

Heavily damaged Henschel Hs 123 A-1, L2+KM from 4.(Schl.)/LG 2, September 1939.

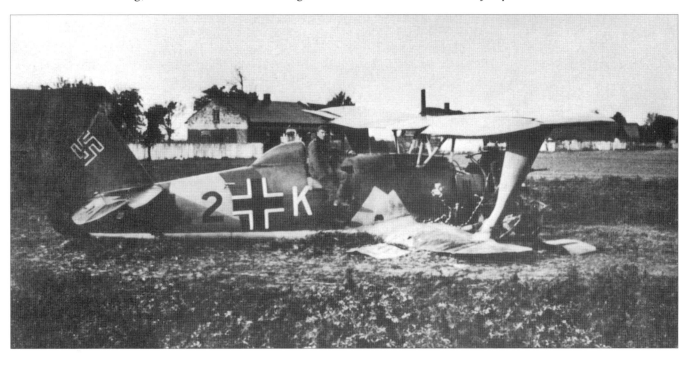

Hs 123 A-1 from 6.(Schl.)/LG 2 in September 1939.

Polish military equipment destroyed at Bzura during attack aircraft raids.

Remnants of the Polish wagons attacked by Hs 123 aircraft while crossing the Bzura River.

on the radio to get the other two flights from our squadron into the area because the target was more than promising!

The flight begins the attack. The aircraft make a wide turn and dive attacking the enemy column from the front. Below, there is incredible confusion. A machine gun rattles, single rifle shots are fired. This weak resistance does not worry us. The ones that fire at us are soon trampled on by troops, horses and vehicles pushing from behind. It is a real mess. The three columns moving alongside are trying to move forward, they ram at each other, the horses bump against one another, the cars crash the transport wagons, the people scatter through the nearby fields, other vehicles crash against the trees at the sides of the road. Gun smoke, dust, exploding ammunition carrying vehicles – horrifying, terrible hell on earth! What is more, the other two flights of our squadron dive for the attack. The countless military column is in the cross fire from our aircraft from the front, rear and both sides. Not many of those on the ground will escape the gruesome fate. There is no sign of anti aircraft artillery. We drop our bombs almost like during training, the whole chaos was caused by almost 300 of them. Between the explosions raising high columns of earth and smoke we hear the fire from our machine guns spitting over 20,000 rounds into the welter of soldiers, horses and vehicles that were ready to fight a short time ago.

The sight is horrible! Destroyed cannons, hundreds of dead horses, scattered transport wagons, broken weapons, dead enemy soldiers. The few lucky ones that escaped the mayhem of the raid are running through the field towards the nearby forest. A horse is galloping, drag-

ging a broken wagon tongue and his wounded companion. The bomb craters are filled with vehicles that fell inside, the frightened horses run over the wounded animals and people. The noise reaches the sky. It is louder than the sound of our engines. When the aircraft gather in the air and make for the home airfield, behind them there is a real desert of terror, a true hell. The hard rule of the war in practice – was it a division or were there more units and equipment destroyed? Nobody knows that, no one shall ask. We are all thinking about their tasks and the mission that was accomplished: The enemy has to be destroyed as long as he seeks the possibility of armed resistance.

The Henschel Hs 123 A-1 proved itself during attacks against withdrawing columns of the Polish Armed Forces.

The 4.(Schl.)/LG 2 emblem containing names of the airfields where the unit was stationed from its creation until the end of the September campaign.

Henschel Hs 123 A-1, W.Nr. 2729, BQ+NL from one of the aviation schools, winter 1939/1940.

Hs 123, GH+NF from the Finsterwalde aviation school.

The Henschel Hs 123 A-1 aircraft from II.(Schl.)/LG 2 on an airstrip in spring of 1940. The aircraft are wearing the pre-war, tri-colour camouflage on the top and side surfaces of the airframe. In the foreground, Messerschmitt Bf 109 E-3 "white 15" from 1./JG 1.

Coming back to our base we already knew: Poland was lost. The people in charge led to its demise. But why is it still fighting?"[15]

In the early morning of 9 September 1939, a lone Fieseler Fi 156C Storch took off from the Wolbórz airfield. The attack squadron commander, Major Spielvogel decided to get to know the course of the front line personally as he had done for many days. Thus he was able to guide his subordinate flights before their combat missions. On that day, it was particularly important as the German tanks were supposed to enter Warsaw.

However, Storch did not return to the home base. In the afternoon, Fw. Zeltner took off to search for the missing commander. According to information provided by the officer of the German panzer unit, the Storch was fired upon, in the area of Okęcie while flying over the front line, probably by the German troops. The pilot, Uffz. Anton Szigora managed to land the aircraft, jumped out of the cockpit evading fire from the enemy. He was hit in the neck and later died in a field hospital. Mortally wounded Maj Spielvogel remained in the cockpit of the shot down Storch.[16]

On that day, at 08.45 the first machines to take off were six Hs 123s from 4. Staffel. After accomplishing their mission near the town of Iłża, they returned the Wolbórz airfield at 09.55.

At 12.51, nine Hs 123s from 5. Staffel took off to bomb targets in east Warsaw. They landed safely at 13.55. Between 14.40 and 15.50, eight Hs 123s of 4. Staffel attacked military columns on the Błonie-Warsaw road. Until the evening the squadron's aircraft flew three more missions against targets on the outskirts Warsaw. While coming back from the combat action, the Hs 123 A, Wn. 2436 was damaged during landing.

On the following day, 10 September 1939, Hptm. Otto Weiß was appointed the new commanding officer of the squadron. As the commander of 5. Staffel he was replaced by Oblt. Grote. The first combat mission was flown by fourteen Hs 123s (seven from 4. and 6. Staffel)

Two Hs 123 A-1 from II.(Schl.)/ LG 2 on the Cambrai airfield. In the background, L2+AC flown by the squadron commander, the Knight's Cross recipient, Hptm. Otto Weiß. Black designation letters, green A with white edging, twin white triangles in the middle part of the top wing, white stripe on the back of the fuselage.

Greetings for soldiers of the British Expeditionary Corps, the sign on the SC 50 bomb under the wing of Hs 123 of II.(Schl.)/LG 2 reads "For the 4.00 o'clock tea".

between 09.15 and 10.30 attacking Polish military columns approaching Warsaw from the north west. From 14.31 to 14.43, nine Hs 123s from 5. Staffel bombed targets at the fork of the road west of Kołbiel.

On 11 September 1939, at 11.20, seven transport Junkers Ju 52/3m aircraft came, bringing Adolf Hitler, Gen.Obst. Wilhelm Keitel, Gen. Obst. Walter von Reichenau and Reichsführer SS Heinrich Himmler along with their entourage. After the meeting with the airmen of the attack squadron, the guests left the airfield at 15.40.

On 12 September 1939, early in the morning, II.(Schl.)/LG 2 flew to the new airfield in Mazowszany. On that day the aircraft did not fly any combat missions.

The next day, the squadron conducted two large operations over Warsaw, in the morning, between 09.55 and 10.58 ten Hs 123s from 5. Staffel took off and in the late afternoon, between 17.11 and 18.20, twenty five aircraft went airborne. During landing at Mazowszany, the Hs 123, Wn. 2251 hit a parked car and was damaged in 50%.

From Thursday 14 September 1939, the command of II.(Schl.)/LG 2 was taken by Maj. Neudörffer. The squadron did not fly any combat missions.

On Friday 15 September 1939, pilots of the attack Hs 123s joined the battle of Bzura. In the morning they bombed Polish positions in the forest north of Jedlińsk and in the afternoon all

Hs 123 A-1 from 5.(Schl.)/LG 2 during the French campaign.

Two Hs 123 A-1s from II.(Schl.)/LG 2 during the campaign in the Western Europe in spring of 1940. In the foreground, 12+- machine with 10+- behind it.

Hs 123 A-1 from II.(Schl.)/LG 2 during the Balkan campaign in April 1941. The entire aircraft is painted with RLM 71 Dunkelgrün, yellow rudder and engine cowling. White Infantry Assault Badge on the sides of the forward part of the fuselage.

three flights operated north of Łowicz escorted by the single engine Messerschmitt Bf 109 Es from 1. and 3./JG 76 patrolling the area west of Sochaczew.

On Sunday 17 September 1939, actions of the attack aircraft were concentrated in the area of Kutno. Along with the Junkers Ju 87Bs from St.G 76 and 77, the Henschel Hs 123 As destroyed bridges and attacked troops crossing the Bzura river to cut the enemy troops on the south bank from supplies and reinforcements. The most effective were again raids against marching columns and transports. The Polish Army Poznań concentrated on a small area became the main target of the attack aircraft and dive bombers in the middle of September 1939. On that day, the squadron flew 117 combat flights. One of the missions was recorded by Curt Strohmeyer: "Combat mission for the attack squadron: 'Attack against Polish military units concentrated in the area of Kutno'. When, according to the orders, we are flying our first mission, the staff swarm, flying in the blue sky at 1,000 metres, gets into heavy anti aircraft fire from Łowicz and has to turn north to evade it. The attack squadron commander used this unplanned manoeuvre to make a reconnaissance of the German bridgehead, at the Vistula river, created at midnight 17 September 1939 to be able to precisely distinguish, during the next operation, the area occupied by our troops. Knowledge of the area occupied by our own units and the detailed information concerning the advance lines is always crucial for the airmen.

The commander marked our units' positions at Wyszogród at the Bzura river estuary and during the return flight noticed some interesting facts: south of Wyszogród, there are three bridge connections at the distance of 10 kilometres. Both northern bridges were busy with traffic going from west to east, mounting

The Henschel 123 A-1 aircraft on one of Greek airfields in spring of 1941, notice the main undercarriage wheels with their fairings removed, yellow rudders and engine cowlings.

Henschel Hs 123 A-1 from 10.(Schl.)/LG 2, red T during the Greek campaign.

on the west side of the Bzura bridges, moreover, there were columns marching from east to west.

The commander immediately ordered the Stab Schwarm to return to base. As always, in our corps, the commander personally leads the staff swarm. Different orders await him at the airfield but the corps headquarters change them on the basis of the commander's report. The squadron is refueled, rearmed and takes off a few minutes later towards the two northern bridges over the Bzura to prevent the Polish divisions, encircled around Kutno, from retreating over the river towards Warsaw. Again we have a huge task to fulfill.

The weather is perfect for the attack pilots. It is easy to spot even the smallest target on the ground. The sun is shining brightly in the endless sky. The blue silk of the sky is mightier and more beautiful for us up here than for those little people on the ground. Initially, our ascending aircraft were casting clear shadows which now become small and very distant but can still be seen. The ground beneath us seems very friendly. When we approach the Bzura, we see clouds of smoke and burning farms. Suddenly our first flight goes in for the attack. A single

– the first dropped bomb! – hits a truck on the northern bridge and one of its pillars simultaneously blocking the bridge. Within a few minutes the southern bridge is destroyed with well aimed bombs. In front of us there are huge masses of infantry, artillery, cavalry, engineers, vehicles of different branches of the armed forces, ammunition transports and all kinds of weapons. The units are stretched through many kilometres in tight columns marching along the roads. When we destroyed both bridges, the enemy had all his retreat routes cut off. Behind them, the cauldron around Kutno, in front the Bzura and Vistula rivers and from the south and south east a strong iron grip of German encirclement; all this makes the escape impossible for the huge mass of troops. Some units try to break from the formation and and get to a safe area with their vehicles and weapons. A heavy defensive fire is directed towards us. So the enemy is capable of fighting and even eager to engage us. It is time to attack.

The attack pilot dives like a Stuka. Aiming the whole aircraft at the target, he opens fire with his machine guns. He tries to hit the opponent in his weakest spot, dropping on him like a bird of prey that cannot let his victim escape.

Henschel Hs 123 A-1, W.Nr. 2732, KB+QA, white 8 from an aviation school.

Another machine from the same school, Hs 123 A-1, KB+QZ, white 20.

Spectacular view of the Henschel Hs 123 A-1 aircraft during a combat flight, four SC 50 bombs attached under the wings, the emblem can be seen on the fuselage – Infanterie Sturmabzeichen (Infantry Assault Badge) painted with white colour.

The squadron divided themselves into swarms and encircled the enemy from all sides. A battery rushes towards the Bzura bridge that is no longer operational, the horses without their coachman fall into the river. Soldiers are running, firing frantically in all directions, towards the Bzura marshes where they get stuck for good. People, animals, everything is jumbled. Horses fall like cut with an axe, dragged by their coaches, others run into the fallen wagons. Somewhere, the whole column is burning with a bright flame. When we are coming in for the second and third run against the enemy, who lost his combat capabilities, the scattered

Close-up of the Hs 123 A-1 cockpit.

Swarm of the Henschel Hs 123 A-1 attack aircraft from 8./Schl.G 1 during operations in the Eastern Front, the machine in the middle is designated with a red letter Q with white edging, painted on the yellow identification stripe.

In the harsh conditions of Russian airfields, the Hs 123 usually operated with the main undercarriage fairings removed, which prevented clogging the wheels with mud and snow.

Adjusting the BMW 132 A-3 engine.

troops are attacked by squadrons of dive bombers that spread death, hell and destruction with their bombs.

Before the enemy had the chance to regroup, he had been beaten, dispelled and rendered defenceless.

Behind us there is nothing but chaos. We are the winners! The attack airmen!"[17]

II.(Schl.)/LG 2 did not fly any combat missions until Wednesday 20 September 1939 when the squadron effectively attacked the enemy units in the area of Sieraków-Wiersze. On Friday 22 September 1939, the squadron aircraft were transferred to the Zalesie airfield.

On Monday 25 September 1939, the Hs 123 As from II.(Schl.)/LG 2 flew 200 combat flights over the Polish capital dropping 800 bombs, 50kg each. Their target was the Ministry of Culture, the Mokotów airfield, power plant and military barracks. Two days later, on 27 September 1939, the squadron operated intensively over the area of the Modlin fortress. Polish anti aircraft artillery shot down one aircraft, the Hs 123 A, Wn 816, its pilot, UffZ. Heinz was not harmed and returned to his unit. It was the third and the last Hs 123 A aircraft lost during the September campaign. All three machines fell victim to Polish anti aircraft artillery.

Oblt. Adolf Galland summed up the participation of the Hs 123 A squadron in the campaign in Poland: "Witin 27 days I flew 50 combat missions. The squadron scored huge success with the loss of only ten men including our commanding officer. In the airfield south of Warsaw, we were visited by Hitler who had a meal with us in the field kitchen, listened to

Infanterie Sturmabzeichen – Infantry Assault Badge, the attack units' emblem painted on the Hs 123 A-1 fuselage.

Aircraft being refueled and armed with bombs on an airfield in Russia.

reports and complemented the course of the operation and the soldiers' conduct."[18]

Campaign in the west

Before the first stage of the German offensive in the west called "Fall Gelb", II.(Schl.)/LG 2 was the part of the VIII. Fliegerkorps still commanded by Gen.Maj. Wolfram von Richthofen. The attack squadron consisted of 50 aircraft of which 45 were airworthy. Since early morning of 10 May 1940, the Henschel Hs 123s took off to attack a grouping of Belgian troops and the areas

of bridges and crossings over the Albert Canal. However, the main task of the attack aircraft was to support the unit of parachute riflemen that landed aboard transport gliders in the area of the Eben-Emael fort securing the bridges over the Albert Canal.

The following day, a group of the Hs 123 As escorted by the Messerschmitt Br 109E fighters, attacked the Belgian airfield near Janeffe, about 10 kilometres west of Liege. During the raid, nine Fairey Fox and one Morane Saulnier M.S. 230 from 5 flight, III Squadron, 1 Regiment of the Belgian Aéronautique Militaire were on the airfield. The German pilots destroyed seven of

Hs 123 A-1s from II./Schl.G 1 prepared for a combat mission.

the nine Fairey Foxes on the ground. In the afternoon of same day, during the attack against the saint Trond airfield, the anti aircraft artillery shot down one Hs 123 A from II.(Schl.)/LG 2. The crippled aircraft tried to land on the runway of the enemy airfield and hit a Belgian Renerd R.31 (side number 7) reconnaissance aircraft that was taking off. The aircraft belonged to 9 flight, V Squadron of the 1 Regiment. Both aircraft were completely destroyed and burned. During the raid of 5.(Schl.)/LG 2 on a military column near Arras, one Hs 123 was attacked by a Hurricane of 607 Squadron piloted by Flt.Lt. George Plinston and sustained 20% damaged.

On the following day, Sunday 12 May 1940, the squadron lost another Henschel that fell victim to a French fighter.

On Monday 13 May 1040, the squadron suffered another loss. The Hs 123 A was shot down at 13.00 near Wavre-Louvain by the British pilot, Sgt. Roy Wilkinson flying the Hurricane fighter (N2353) from the RAF 3 Squadron.

On the next day, a dozen or so Hs 123 As escorted by a swarm of the Bf 109Es from II./JG 2 were attacked by Hurricanes from the RAF 242 and 607 Squadrons, near Louvain. The Brit-

ish, outnumbering the Henschels, shot down two Hs 123 As from 5.(Schl.)/LG 2, their pilots: Uffz. Karl-Siegfried Lückel and Lt. Georg Ritter survived. They were both found by the advance Wehrmacht panzer units and returned to their unit. Three of the attacking Hurricanes were shot down by the pilots of II./JG 2 and the fourth one by two Hs 123 As that managed to outmanoeuvre the opponent and get him in the crossfire of their machine guns![19]

On the same day, the Luftwaffe attack squadron lost another machine shot down by the anti aircraft artillery over Tirlemont, south east of Louvain. The pilot, Lt. Georg Dörffel of 5. Staffel was lightly wounded but managed to emergency land and soon returned to his unit.[20]

On 15 May 1940, the unit was transferred to the Duras airfield from where it flew close support missions for the tanks of the 6 Army.

After Brussels had been captured on 17 May 1940, VIII. Fliegerkorps was placed under the command of the Luftflotte 3. Its main task was to support the tanks from the Panzergruppe von Kleist that were moving through the territory of Luxemburg and the Ardennes towards the English Channel. The Henschel 123 As actively supported the German engineers while crossing the Meuse river and later participated in the battle of Sedan.

On 18 May 1040, the commanding officer of II.(Schlacht)/LG 2, Hptm. Otto Weiß, was the first attack aircraft pilot to receive the Knight's Cross.[21]

After the front line had reached the vicinity of Dunkirk and the banks of the Channel, II.(Schl.)/LG 2 was moved to the Cambrai airfield on 21 May 1940. On the following day, near Amiens, a strong group of Allied tanks began their counter attack against the weak German flank. Obstlt. Hans Seidemann, the chief of staff of the VIII. Fliegerkorps, who at that

Henschel Hs123 A-1, black B with white edging from II./Schl.G 1 during mission in the Eastern Front.

time was at the Cambrai airfield, immediately ordered all airworthy attack aircraft and dive bombers to take off. At that moment, a damaged reconnaissance Heinkel He 46 biplane appeared over the airfield. It did not even attampt to land but lowered its altitude and the observer dropped a report: "About 40 enemy tanks and 150 trucks with infantry are advancing towards Cambrai from the north". The report made the officers realize the scale of the threat. Cambrai was the key supply point of the panzer corps whose main forces were already near the banks of the English Channel. At that moment, the hinterland town did not have any anti tank means. The only weapon that could threaten the enemy tanks was a battery of anti aircraft guns positioned around the airfield and the squadron of the Henschel 123 A attack aircraft.

The first to take off were four Stab Henschels. Hptm. Otto Weiß entered the cockpit of the first machine. After a few minutes flight, sixteen kilometres from the airfield, first enemy tanks could be seen. As Hptm. Weiß remembers: "The tanks were preparing for the attack in groups of four to six machines gathering on the south side of the de la Sensée canal while, on its north side we could see a long column of trucks approaching."[22]

The four Henschels, without delay, attacked the enemy dropping bombs and strafing the targets. After the attack, Hptm. Weiß radioed all squadron pilots to gather for operational briefing.

Immediately after the briefing, the Henschels took off again. They continued to do so for almost an hour. The attack aircraft were escorted by the Messerschmitt Bf 109Es from I./JG 21 and I./JG 51 that effectively repelled attacks of numerous Allied fighters. During the first raids the attack pilots managed to destroy about 20 tanks, however the remaining ones kept on moving towards Cambrai. They were soon stopped by direct fire from the highly effective 88mm Flak 18 anti aircraft guns of the XXXIII. Flak-Regiment that constituted the air-

The most famous Hs 123 pilot, recipient of the Knight's Cross, Lt. Josef „Bazi" Menapace, commanding officer of 7./Schl.G 1.

Lt. Menapace and his Hs 123 B-1, above the II./Schl.G 1 emblem, white inscription „Rolf v. Zahradnicek".

Hs 123 A-1, PF+UV, white 7 from Ergänzungsstaffel/Schl.G 1 combat training unit in summer 1942 on the Novotcherkask airfield.

field's security forces. Within a few minutes, five tanks were burning and the remaining ones withdrew.

On 5 June 1940, the second act of the western campaign began. The operation "Fall Rot" with aim to completely destroy the French army and capture the rest of the French territory. The first day of the operation brought the loss of three II.(Schl.)/LG 2 aircraft. The first one was shot down by French fighters from GC I/6, the second one crashed at the Puisieux airfield and the third one was destroyed after the engine fire.

The actions were described by Curt Strohmeyer: "The attack squadron is stationed south of Soissons in Daumiers. For the first time the weather is not favourable. It is cloudy and these clouds are not pilot friendly. For now, it is not that bad. We landed after the mission executed in the force of the whole squadron and we are looking forward to an hour of rest. After

a while our flight gets an operational order: 'Pursue the enemy...'

The cloud base over the airfield is at 300 metres. We do not know what the situation is like in the target area and that is why the flight received an order, from the commanding officer to break off the attack in case of low cloud base. Our flight consisting of two swarms takes off again to face the enemy.

The weather is getting worse. 120km from the airfield, the cloud base is as low as 200 metres and then descends to 100 metres. We feel like in the laundry house, surrounded by steam. Soon visibility is close to zero as the cloud base gets even lower. It is understandable why the flight commander decides to abort the mission. The second swarm, during the return flight, looses contact with the commander's swarm and when the clouds almost touch the ground, the formation breaks completely. The swarm

Two Hs 123 A-1s, white 1 and white 2, CA+ZY from Ergänzungsstaffel/Schl.G 1.

Henschel Hs 123 A-1, from one of the training units, with external fuel tank under the fuselage.

commander and his wingman are now on their own. So, north they go! Both aircraft are flying along the valley. Because visibility is almost none, they are looking for a place to land and simultaneously they are trying to recognize the terrain. It is not easy since they do not know where the enemy is and landing is not only dangerous for the pilot, but also for the machine that is needed for further combat missions.

But they can see an airfield! It seems deserted. It is probably a French military airfield that had been evacuated. The swarm commander lands, moves smoothly along the field and turns the aircraft slightly to the side. He parks the machine an looks for his wingman who is now on the landing approach. Than, his heart stops. His colleague's machine touches down and disappears in a horrific explosion that lifts

The unexpected attack of winter in November 1942 hampered the maintenance of the II./Schl.G 1 aircraft.

The Hs 123 aircraft from II./ Schl.G 1 in winter 1942 near Stalingrad.

the fuselage five or more metres into the air. The remains of the torn aircraft fall into a huge cloud of smoke. The swarm commander jumps out of his aircraft to look for his companion who is probably already dead.. However, the lucky man stands up from the wreckage of his machine, apparently without a scratch, looking dazedly around the airfield that gave him such a warm welcome.

It is not hard to guess that the whole place was mined and the Leutnant had tonnes of luck landing his aircraft and parking it safely at the

side of the airfield. He is fully aware of the fact. The Unteroffizier is indeed unharmed. He was not even scratched during the accident. What a stroke of luck!

Now it is time to look at the map to find out where they are. The Leutnant and his wing-man agree that they have to return to base before the tomorrow combat actions begin. However it will not be that easy. They managed to define the direction where the Henschel should fly but there was another serious problem. The trusty Henschel Hs 123 attack aircraft was

Henschel 123 A-1 in winter camouflage, covered with white, easy-to-wash paint.

Hs 123 A-1, yellow E from 7./
Schl.G 1 in the south sector
of the Eastern Front.

a single seater with no possibility to take passengers aboard. But now, the other person had to fit in. After a while, the Leutnant decided to tie the Unteroffizier to the fuselage and take him back to the base. The blast of air will surely make him a little cold but it was important to come back to the home airfield on time before the next mission! Both airmen started to look for something to tie the NCO. The did not have suspenders, just two belts, a few leather straps and a short line. The Unteroffizier sat on the fuselage just behind the engine cowling. The Leutnant started to tie him to the wing struts so even the strongest blast of wind could not blow him down. All knots double checked, it was time to think about the hardest part of the return flight. How to take off not hitting any mines?

There were a clear wheel marks on the grass of the airfield. The Leutnant followed it checking the ground around it. The French must have forgotten to place mines where he landed. However, where the wheel tracks ended, countless mines could be seen, every square metre was a deadly trap. Not every day is so lucky! Under no circumstances could the taking off aircraft move further than the touch down mark. It was damn risky! The Unteroffizier was crouching in the prop blast. The aircraft started to move forward. The take off manoeuvre began. The engine roared at full power, the machine rushed forward. The Leutnant had marked the take off point with a stick that he had driven into the ground and now had to observe it carefully. The machine was moving faster and faster. Is there enough take off space before the mine field? Blood was rushing through the pilot's veins, pulsing in the ears. He was expecting an explosion. Finally, the aircraft went airborne and after a while landed on the home airfield.

The Leutnant immediately reported to the command officer: "Two pilots and one aircraft reporting for duty."[23]

During the first week of fighting, the attack squadron supported the 6 and 9 Army that, after crossing the Marne river, were moving towards Paris. The pilots mainly flew missions against the enemy counter attacks. One of the actions was described by war correspondent, Curt Strohmeyer: "The squadron commander leaned over the map, his Knight's Cross was slowly swinging above the table. He pointed at the direction of Montmiral between Esternay and Sezanne, more or less where our panzer units had to attack. One of the squadron's flights was to be used as close air support for the advancing tanks. The task was difficult, as the pace of the panzer units' advance was really fast and it was hard to determine their location. The forward units not always had the possibility to mark themselves for the air observers. What was hard to believe, about the afternoon, the tanks broke into the enemy positions, far

Henschel Hs 123 A-1, W.Nr.
2325, red H from II./Schl.G 1.

Hs 123 A-1, W.Nr. 2303, CA+AW, white 25 from Stuka Vorschule 1, Bad Aibling 1941.

Another view of the same aircraft. In the cockpit, August Diemer, who later became the 8./St.G 77 ace, recipient of the German Cross in Gold with over 600 combat missions flown.

that was attempting to flank the German units. Using the confusion on the ground our aircraft strafed the columns with their machine guns breaking the enemy formation and limiting their combat efficiency practically to zero.

The tanks kept on attacking, moving towards Romilly. The attack squadron conducted three more raids, every time protecting the left flank of the panzer units. During the return flight from the first operation, the Stab swarm moved away from the rest of the formation and, south of Esternay, near Montmort-Vertus-Etoges, spotted a large enemy column consisting of three or four regiments. Our own infantry crossed the Meuse river at Dormans and moved deep into the enemy positions. The attack squadron had another task to fulfill: To destroy the strong enemy group and prevent it from holding back German troops and counterattacking, from the south west, the flank of our panzer forces positioned far south from Sezanne.

The attack airmen executed the task in the best possible way. They attacked the enemy columns three times with all available aircraft. During the raids we bombed all formations concentrating on numerous horse-drawn vehicles. That caused the confusion on the ground turn into a real disaster. The middle of the road was blocked by the whole artillery battery as we had shot all the horses. Along the whole column, we saw similar scenes of destruction and defeat. The enemy formation posed no more threat for our troops!

On the following day, the panzers crossed the Seine river and we provided cover on both their flanks. Again, on the other Seine bank, we encountered numerous enemy columns moving along all roads leading south. The columns

behind the Esternay-Sezanne line. The situation was perfect for the attack squadron as the enemy, withdrawing south from the area of Esternay-Chalons sur Marne, was trying to make a turn and threaten the Sezanne flank of the panzer forces. The attack squadron's task was to cover the left flank of the tank units.

During the first operation conducted in the afternoon, the squadron encountered strong enemy units marching south in the centre and east of the town of Sezanne. The aircraft immediately dived and effectively dropped their bombs that stopped the enemy's advance party

marched in tight formations presenting a perfect target for the attack aircraft. We attacked the columns four times and destroyed everything that was not dispersed and did not escape. In every raid we dropped bombs and during three missions strafed the targets. Not a single enemy column dared to cross the Seine to the west and no column was able to turn south as it would immediately become a target for our attack pilots. The dispersed units were not able to continue their march in tight formations. Sometimes the enemy, thinking the danger had passed, tried to regroup to keep on moving but their units were observed from the air and immediately attacked which caused panic in the new formations and broke the soldiers mentally. Their combat strength and discipline went down the drain. It was a real disaster.

Panzers advanced with such speed that the range of our aircraft was not enough to provide effective air support. It was not a big problem. On the next day, the squadron, after a few operations, landed on one of the captured and repaired airfields."[24]

The squadron suffered its last combat loss on 15 June 1940 when French fighters shot down one Hs 123 A.

As Curt Strohmeyer reports: "On 17 June the attack squadron was transferred to the Auxerre operational airfield. We flew one combat mission over Chatillons but we encountered only our own troops. After we landed, the squadron's staff adjutant said laughing: 'If it continues, we will have to believe that the infantry can march faster than we fly!' Soon after that, we flew our last mission in France, in bad weather conditions.

It was 17 June 1940. Dijon capitulated in the afternoon. Despite of that fact, a French division was marching from the north west towards Dijon with the intention to recapture the city. The attack squadron was informed that our units had already attacked the advance troops of the division. We decided to take care of the main forces of the division that were not in combat contact with our troops. We managed to disperse the enemy and partially destroy its forces. Everything went on like in training exercise and did not take much time. We arrived at the battlefield according to plan, executed the task without a single loss, assembled into a formation and returned to Auxere. Our last operation prevented the French division from attacking Dijon. All regiments constituting the division were later taken prisoner by our troops. It was not a difficult task since most of the soldiers were very disordered and in panic which was the result of our bombing and strafing runs."[25]

After the conclusion of the western campaign, II.(Schl.)/LG 2 was withdrawn to the

Braunschweig base where two of the three flights of the squadron were rearmed with the Messerschmitt Bf 109E-7/B fighter bombers. Then the squadron was transferred to the Böblingen airfield, the home of the fighter bomber school.

"Operation Marita" – the Balkan operations

On Sunday, 6 April 1941 at 05.15 the German troops crossed the borders of Yugoslavia and Greece. Close air support for the Wehrmacht units was provided by the aircraft of the 4 Air Fleet. The fleet included the VIII. Fliegerkorps along with II.(Schl.)/LG 2 whose one flight stationed in the Sofia-Wrażdebna base was armed with The Henschel 123 As. The same aircraft were used by 10./LG 2 stationed at the Krainici airfield in Bulgaria.

At dawn, on 6 April 1941 the Bf 109Es and Hs 123 As from II.(Schl.)/LG 2 took off from the Sofia-Wrażdebna airfield. Their target was the base of the 35 Fighter Regiment of the Royal Yugoslav Air Force (35. Lovacka Vazduhoplovna Puk, Jugoslovensko Kraljevsko Ratno Vazduhoplovstwo – JKRV), the Rezanovacka Kosa airfield. Before the German aircraft reached the target area, the Yugoslav Hawker Fury fighters had already been airborne. The Hs 123 As managed to destroy only one Fury fighter on the ground, three training planes and one RWD 13 liaison aircraft made in Poland. All 11 Yugoslav biplanes were shot down by the Messerschmitt 109 Es.

After 08.00 the Hs 123 As took off again, this time to bomb the defensive positions of

Two generations of German attack aircraft, in the air – a swarm of Hs 123s, on the ground – Fw 190s ready for take off.

The Henschel 123 A-1 aircraft from 4./SG 2 in late spring of 1944. In the foreground, W.Nr. 0846 marked with a yellow letter L.

Hs 123 A-1, W.Nr. 0846 with the SC 50 bombs equipped with the "Dinort's rods".

the Yugoslav army at Stracin, about 40km from the border. Uffz. Hanneberg had a stroke of bad luck when his aircraft was hit by an unfortunate single round, fired from a rifle. It burst into flames and the pilot had to land. Hanneberg was captured.

Within the next few days, due to bad weather conditions, the German air force was not very active. On 12 April 1941, German troops entered Belgrade and Zagreb. Although the fighting would continue until 21 April, the campaign had already been won and the VIII. Fliegerkorps units were moved to operations against Greece.

On 19 April 1941, the aircraft of II.(Schlsht)/LG 2 attacked the Amphiklia/Lodi airfield where beside the Greek PZL P-24G and Bloch M.B. 151, the British Gloster Gladiator biplanes were stationed. One Hs 123 A was slightly damaged by anti aircraft fire.

The Henschel 123 As operated over Greece until the end of April 1941 providing close air support for the German troops fighting at the Corinth Canal.

Operation Barbarossa – the attack on the Soviet Union

Only 17 airworthy Henschel 123 As of the total of 22 aircraft of II.(Schl.)/LG 2 participated in the attack against the Soviet Union which started at dawn on 22 June 1941. The squadron was stationed at the Praszniki airfield near the Lithuanian border. The squadron was part of the VIII. Fliegerkorps operationally subordinate to the Luftflotte 2. The task of the VIII. Air Corps was to support the panzer and mechanized units of the Panzergruppe 3.

The Henschel 123 As took part in the first strike against Soviet airfields located at the border and destroyed no less than 1,489 enemy aircraft. Then, the attack aircraft provided close air support for panzer units during the encirclement operation near Białystok and Mińsk.

At the beginning of August 1941, the unit was transferred north with a task to support the Panzergruppe 4 heading towards Leningrad. At the end of September 1941, the squadron was moved to the middle sector of the front line and participated in the battles of Vyazma and Briańsk. In October 1941, II.(Schl.)/LG 2 was stationed at the Kalinin airfield where the scenario from a year ago, when the Hs 123 A pilots had to defend the base against the attack of French tanks, repeated itself. This time, the Soviet attack was stopped only at the edge of the airfield. Maj. Otto Weiß, commanding the defence, was given an honourable nickname by his soldiers, „Der Löwe von Kalinin" (The Lion of Kalinin). With the beginning of the Russian winter all Luftwaffe activity seized. Although, according to the chief constructor of the Henschel company, CE Nicolaus, the Hs 123 A: "...as the only Luftwaffe aircraft, during the 1941/42 winter, was able to execute attack missions from the Eastern Front airfields covered with deep snow"[26], low temperatures also grounded the Henschel 123s which were withdrawn to Germany.

At the beginning of 1942, in Werl near Dortmund, the first attack regiment of the Luftwaffe, Schlachtgeschwader 1 (Schl.G 1) was created on the basis of II.(Schl.)/LG 2. The unit included two squadrons of four flights each. One flight of each squadron was armed with the Henschel 123 A aircraft. Maj. Otto Weiß was appointed the commanding officer of the regiment.

Eastern Front 1942-1944

During the period of forming and training of Schl.G 1, power plants, fuel and oil installations of all Henschel 123 As were modified to prepare the aircraft for the harsh conditions of the Russian winter. Another modification was the addition of headrests on the back of the fuselage, to protect the pilot's head in case of a nose-over, to earlier versions of the aircraft built without that feature. Apart from that, using the spare parts and components, ten additional Hs 123 As were assembled. At the beginning of May 1942. after the training had been completed, Schl.G 1 was transferred to the Eastern Front to the Grammatikowo airfield at Crimea where it became part of the Luftflotte 4. The airfield was situated on the Kerch Peninsula in the centre

section of the front line. While fending off the Soviet attacks, the unit lost four aircraft.

At the end of May 1942, the Hs 123 As participated in the battle of Kharkov were Hptm. Josef Menapace became famous for his fights effective actions Soviet armour. After commencing the "Fall Blau" operation, the German summer offensive in the south section of the Eastern Front, the Henschel 123 As continued their close air support actions which earned them a nickname "Obergefreiter" (Senior Lance-Corporal), given to them by their comrades from the ground forces.

Hs 123 A-1, W.Nr. 0846 on the air strip, a fragment of yellow letter L and black chevron can be seen on the fuselage.

Losses of the Henschel 123 A aircraft from Schl.G 1 between 1 January to to 31 August 1942					
Date	Wn.	Flight	Pilot	Pilot's fate	Remarks
20.01.1942	0969	8.	-	-	Dugino, hit an obstacle, 50%
07.02.1942	0794	8.	Lt. Rolf von Zahradnicek	Killed	Near Okovokovo, anti aircraft artillery, 100%
13.02.1942	2256	8.	Unknown	-	Near Sychevka, emergency landing due to damages caused by anti aircraft defence, 20%
26.02.1942	2345	8.	Unknown	-	Dugino, emergency landing due to engine failure, 25%
01.03.1942	0832	8.			Dugino airfield, enemy air raid, 30%
01.03.1942	0632	8.			Dugino airfield, enemy air raid, 50%
04.03.1942	2274	8.	Unknown		Dugino, emergency landing due to damages caused by anti aircraft defence, 40%
06.03.1942	2302	8.			Dugino airfield, enemy air raid, 90%
08.03.1942	2270	I.	Unknown		Witebsk, emergency landing due to engine failure 30%
17.03.1942	2284	8.			Dugino, damaged while taxiing, 70%
05.04.1942	0971	8.			Dugino, during landing rammed a Ju 87, 50%
14.04.1942	2336	I.			Wyazma, undercarriage damage due to faulty maintenance, 20%
16.04.1942	2291	I.			Stabna, enemy fighter fire, 100%
12.05.1942	2271	7.			?
13.05.1942	2285	7.		No injuries	Near Marhovką, enemy fire, 100%
17.05.1942	2426	7.			Konstantinovka airfield, during taxiing, 10%
29.06.1942	0939	7.		No injuries	Near Ludrey, anti aircraft artillery fire, 100%
29.06.1942	2332	7.	Lt. Hans Stenkamp	Killed	Schtschigry, unknown cause, 100%
29.06.1942	2431	7.	Uffz. Heinrich Klein	killed	Schtschigry, unknown cause, 100%
29.06.1942	2333	7.	Uffz. Paul Ranstätter	No injuries	Schtschigry, unknown cause, 100%
15.07.1942	2434	1.			Poltava, engine failure, 80%
16.07.1942	2248	7.			Suchinevka, nose-over during landing, 50%
30.07.1942	0858	7.			Near Wenzy, enemy fire, 90%
30.07.1942	2344	7.			2927 sector, emergency landing due to engine failure, 30%
03.08.1942	0211	5.			Froloff-West airfield, accidental bomb explosion, 60%
05.08.1942	0855	7.			2927 sector, ground fire, 100%
06.08.1942	0223	II.			4974 sector, anti aircraft artillery fire, 100%

The basic bomb armament of the Hs 123 A-1 were the SC 50 and AB 70 bombs.

On 20 August 1942, Hptm. Josef "Bazi" Menapace, promoted to 7. Staffel commander on 31 July 1942, flew his 650th mission at the controls of the Henschel Hs 123 and received the Knight's Cross. On 13 September 1942, during heavy fighting at Stalingrad, his Hs 123 A-1, Wn. 2250 was shot down by Soviet fighters. Hptm. Menapace survived and managed to return to his unit.

At that time, the aircraft of II./Schl.G 1 were operating from the Oblivskaya airfield. Heavy frost, in the first part of November 1942, made the Hs 123 A actions difficult. The pilots, despite wearing electrically heated flight suits, were subjected to changeable weather conditions. When the warm front approached in the second half of November 1942, the weather conditions deteriorated with fog, heavy snowfall and sleet. The Russians took advantage of German inability to fly reconnaissance missions and launched a counter offensive to encircle Stalingrad and cut the German 6 Army off the main forces. With the progress of the Soviet army, 7./Schl.G 1 had to withdraw further west. After leaving the Oblivskaya airfield, the unit moved to Morozovskaya, then to Millerevo and finally Voroshilovgrad. At the end of January 1943, the Hs 123s operated mainly over Donets. Fter the 6 Army capitulated in Stalingrad, II./Schl.G 1 was sent to be reinforced to the Dęblin-Irena base.

In April 1943, the unit returned to the front. I was sent to Kuban where it supported the 17 Army desperately defending the bridgehead. The Soviet forces had large numbers of fighter aircraft which made matters worse for the slow Hs 123. For the first time, large quantities of Soviet attack aircraft appeared. They frequently attacked the Anapa base where II./Schl.G 1 was stationed. During one of the raids, on 19 April 1943, the Soviet attack aircraft destroyed two Henschel 123 As on the ground, Wn. 2333 and 0333.

In July 1943, 21 Hs 123 A aircraft fro II./Schl.G 1 provided air support during the last German offensive in the east, in the area of Kursk. After the "Zitadelle" operation, the Hs 123 flight was moved to the Rudka airfield from where it flew to defend Kharkov. In September 1943 the number of airworthy aircraft dropped down to seven. On 18 October 1943 the Luftwaffe attack units were reorganized and their designations changed. II./Schl.G 1 was renamed II./SG 2. At that time, the front units had, on average, 10-12 airworthy Hs 123 aircraft that were withdrawn in the first half of 1944.

In foreign service

Spain

In August 1937, two Henschel Hs 123 As designated 24●3 i 24●5 that had been in service in Stuka 88 of the Legion Condor were handed over to the Spanish Air Force (Aviación Nacional). Both aircraft were named "Angelitos" and they were piloted by Capitán Antonio Bazán Martinez, Teniente Antonio Garcia Delgado, Alférez Mariano Varona Trigueros and Alférez José Velaz de Medrano Echevarria.[27] The reserve pilots were Capitán José Guitar Rodrigez, Alférez Emilio Ugarte Ruiz and Alférez Alfonso de Vierna Pita.

The Spanish Hs 123 As operated from the Cordoba and Posadas airfields. At the end of 1937, they were transferred to the Alfaro and Bello airfields from where they supported the nationalist forces during fights in the area of Teruel. At the turn of January and February 1938, the aircraft were moved to southern front in Andalusia. In February 1938, the Spanish Hs 123 As cooperated with the German Ju 87 A-1 dive bombers during raids against republican positions at Teruel. In spring and summer of 1938, "Angelitos" were operating along with the Aero A-101 "Ocas" from Grupo 5-G-17. They were used so intensively that both airframes were soon unable to perform any actions. At the end of 1938, the aircraft were sent to the Granada and Calzadilla de los Barros airbases as completely unfit for flying. The pilots flying the Hs 123 A were sent to other units.

The aircraft standing inactively caught the attention of Alférez Antonio Paris Granados and Alférez Pedro Beca from Grupo Mixto 86-70 who managed to persuade their unit commander to try and revive both planes. The two attack aircraft would be a great asset of Escuadrilla 4-E-10 of Grupo Mixto 86-70 where both young pilots served. Their unit had a huge variety of equipment – a few Heinkel He 70 F "Rayos", two Junkers 86 D "Jumos" and one captured Tupolev SB-2 "Katiuska".

During the overhaul, it turned out that the electrical generators powering the underwing bomb release mechanisms could not be repaired. Because original spare parts were impossible to obtain, the mechanics replaced the German electrical bomb release system with a Spanish Santiago Mendi mechanical system used to release 70kg fragmentation bombs. The bombs were fitted with one metre long rods that activated the fuse on impact. The bomb would explode a few dozen centimetres above the ground thus enlarging its kill zone. A similar solution was used by the German Luftwaffe during World War II.

The repairs and modifications of both Hs 123 As were successful and the aircraft were deployed to Gupo Mixto 86-70 actively participating in combat missions. On 23 December 1938, Alférez Pedro Beca piloting one of the machines, noticed a republican military transport at the Martos train station. He started diving from 1,200 metres and released the first of four bombs at 600 metres. Almost immediately he felt a shock that turned into strong vibrations. Surprised, he performed an emergency release the remaining bombs and nursed his aircraft to the base. From the cockpit, he was not able to determine the cause of vibrations but the aircraft kept flying so he decided to try to reach the Castro del Rio airfield 30km away. After a few minutes flight he managed to land at the edge of his home airfield.

When on the ground, it became clear that the first bomb had hit a propeller blade and damaged it. The Henschel 123 A was not fitted with air brakes, so the bomb released in a dive, flew beside the aircraft for a while, before overtaking it on its way towards the ground. One of the bomb's stabilizers that must have been bent, changed the bomb's direction causing it to hit the propeller blade.

The aircraft was repaired provisionally on the spot. The mechanics replaced the original propeller with the Junkers Ju 52/3m prop and sent the machine for an overhaul to the Tablada base. Since the accident had become known around Spain, a ground crew of the Legion Condor also arrived at Tablada to inspect the aircraft.

On 31 March 1939, the Spanish war was over. Soon, Aviación Nacional received another 12 Hs 123 A-1 aircraft from Germany. The price of one machine was 86,511.33RM.[28] Along with the "old" Hs 123 As the aircraft were deployed to Grupo 24 stationed in Tablada, commanded by Capitán Fernando Martinez Mejías.

In September 1939 the unit was renamed to Escuadrilla de bombardeo en picado.[29] Its new commanding officer became Capitán Antonio Sanz Garcia Veas. On 19 December the unit was renamed to 61° Escuadrilla.

Refueling the fuselage tank of the Hs 123 A-1.

On 20 february 1940, the Spanish Ministry of Aviation, don Juan Yagüe asked Generalissimo Francisco Franco for permission to sell all Hs 123 A-1 aircraft abroad. To justify his request he stated that the number of spare parts was so small that in case of an armed conflict, the aircraft would not be able to remain active for more than two months. Despite the approval, the aircraft were so outdated that it was impossible to find a buyer, so the machine remained in service with the Spanish Air Force.

In 1941 two of them were destroyed in crashes, the first one, Hs 123 A-1, 24●17 crashed on 3 October during training flight near Baños del Carmen close to Malaga. Its pilot, Alférez Manuel Esteban Gonzáles was killed. The other one, side number 24●13 had a mid-air collision with the Bücker Bü 131 B (33●103) on 5 November. Both pilots were killed.

On 1 December, the Henschel 123 A-1 received new Spanish air force designation – BV.1 (Bombardero Vertical, tipo 1). On 21 March 1946, the Henschel 123 A-1 aircraft that were still in active duty were moved to the Alcalá de Henares airfield in Madrid and became part of 11° Grupo Regimento Mixto No 1. The last Hs 123 A-1 in service of Ejército del Aire Español[30] was the BV.1-3 with side number 33●55 that flew until the end of 1952 in 33° Grupo at the Villanubla airfield near Valladolid. While taxiing, Capitán Mena Urdangarin hit a pole and tore off right horizontal stabilizer. Because the repair was cost-ineffective the aircraft was scrapped.

China

After the Sino-Japanese war broke out in July 1937, the Chinese government launched efforts to find equipment for the air force. The Chinese government representatives arrived in Germany where they ordered 12 Henschel 123 A-1 aircraft in the Henschel Flugzeugwerke AG in Belinie-Schönefeld. The Reich's Ministry of

Defence agreed to sell the aircraft that were initially to be purchased by Portugal. The price of 168,133,33RM[31] was not too high for the Chinese military.

On 3 November 1937, in China, representatives of the German Deutsche Handelsgesellschaft für industrielle Produkte (HAPRO) company[32] taking care of arms trade for the Reich, signed a contract for a delivery of 12 Hs 123 A-1 aircraft along with spare parts for the total of 2,017,600RM. The aircraft were to be received on 22 November 1937 in Schönefeld . Then, on 26 November they were to be loaded aboard a ship in Bremen and sent to Hong Kong.

For political reasons, the delivery was delayed for a month. The boxes with disassembled aircraft were accompanied by a delegation of the Henschel company workers – 13 assembly workers directed by von Winterfeldt – an officer of the Luftwaffe reserve, the test pilot of the company whose task was to test fly the machines after their assembly in China. The delegation was joined by two technicians, Brauske who was responsible for power plants and hydraulics and Walter Neff, electronics, radio and armament expert. After unloading, the boxes with aircraft parts took a long journey to the north of China, to the city of Hankau, near Wuhan at the Yangtze river. In the middle of January 1939, the Chinese workers supervised by the German specialists, began the assembly of the aircraft. A large wooden hangar was used as the assembly room. The aircraft were then test flown and handed over to the Chinese pilots. Soon it turned out that they lacked the necessary experience. And soon, an accident happened. During landing, one of the Chinese pilots noticed a man crossing the runway, pulled the aircraft up for a second approach but forgot to retract the flaps he had extended for landing. The aircraft was not able to gain speed, landed very hard and with high speed moved towards the hangar, hit one of its

Hs 123 A-1 with the SD 50 bombs.

walls and seriously damaged the top wing. Because a spare wing was at hand, the aircraft was soon restored to its original condition.

In April 1938, the assembly of all twelve aircraft was concluded. The machines were test flown until the middle of May. Because every aircraft was painted with the RLM 02 Grau on all surfaces, the Chinese completed the camouflage with small green snake-shaped lines painted on top and side surfaces of the airframe.[33] Tactical numbers from 1501 to 1512 were painted on the vertical stabilizer. Nine aircraft (from 1501 to 1509) were deployed to 15 squadron of the Chinese Air Force, three (1510-1512) were kept in reserve. The Chinese Hs 123 A-1s served on the front line for eighteen months until the end of 1939. During six months of their service, the aircraft executed at least three raids against Japanese inland ships on the Yangtze river. After withdrawing from front line duties , several Hs 123 A-1s were used as training aircraft in 6 Chinese Fighter Regiment.

Unrealized export plans

In the second half of the 1930s, Austria began the third phase of rearming and modenizing its military aviation. These actions were based on the purchase of military equipment from Germany. Hptm. Johann Schalk of Fliegerregiment Nr 2[34] was authorized to test all types of German aircraft, the purchase of which was taken under consideration by the Austrian aviation. On 6 November 1937, along with representatives of the military aviation, he went on a three-week trip around Germany where he visited aviation factories in Berlin, Bremen, Dessau, Rostock and Köthen. The Austrian delegation was particularly interested in fighter aircraft like the Heinkel He 112, reconnaissance Henschel Hs 126 and Junkers Ju 87 dive bombers.

As a competition for the Ju 87, Hptm. Schalk also test flew the Henschel Hs 123 A over the Berlin-Schönefeld airport. The aircraft had civilian designation D-INVI. After the test flight, Schalk prepared a detailed report. As a conclusion he stated that the Hs 123 A was not a typical dive bomber but it could serve as a fighter and a close air support aircraft.[35] The single seat Henschel turned out to be more manoeuvrable than the Ju 87 two seater, but it could only take 250kg of bombs[36]. The outdated construction, small bomb load and the preference for a dive bomber over an attack aircraft made the Austrians order twelve Junkers Ju 87 As and waive the Henschel 123 A.

However, neither the twelve ordered Stukas, twelve Henschel 126s or 42 Heinkel He 112s were delivered to the Austrians as on 13 March 1938 the Republic of Austria was annexed by the Third Reich.

At the end of the 30s of the 20th century, Portugal also wanted to modernize its air force. Arma de Aeronáutica was very much interested in new bombers and attack aircraft. The interest was a result of the Spanish war experience where a military mission – Missão Militar de Observação em Espanha (M.M.P.O.E.) – was sent sent by the Portuguese.

Because Antonio Salazar's government was on good terms with the Italian and German governments, representatives of the Portuguese air force paid a series of visits in Italy and Germany where they inspected the factories of Arado, Focke-Wulf, Henschel, Junkers and Messerschmitt.

After ordering the transport Junkers Ju 52/3m and the Junkers Ju 86K bombers, the command of the Portuguese air force announced a competition for a close air support aircraft. Three constructions entered the competition: Italian Breda Ba.65, Henschel Hs 123 A and Polish P.Z.L. P.23 Karaś.

All three aircraft were test flown by Major António de Sousa Maya, the Great War veteran, the commanding officer of the Grupo Independente de Aviação de Protecção e Combate stationed in Tancos.[37] During testing, the Polish P.Z.L. P.23 Karaś proved to be a very durable construction and a stable weapons platform but it was not able to drop bombs in a dive which excluded it from the competition. The Henschel Hs 123 received the highest marks after it had proven its excellent flying capabilities and easy maintenance, even in difficult field conditions.

Despite higher performance than the Italian Breda Ba.65 dive bomber and the advanced negotiations to purchase of 12 Hs 123 aircraft, the Portuguese prime minister Antonio Salazar decided to buy the bombers in Italy. The decision was affected by political calculations concerning the will to tighten the cooperation with Benito Mussolini. The purchase was finalized, but the Breda Ba.65 aircraft turned out to be quite unreliable and the Portuguese had to face many problems with its operation.

Technical description

The Henschel Hs 123 A-1 was a single seat sesquiplane with metal structure, powered by the nine-cylinder, radial BMW 132A-3 engine with maximum power of 632hp. The cylinder had a diameter of 155.5mm, 162mm stroke, 3.076dm³ capacity and 1:6 compression ratio. The engine was mounted on a cradle of steel tubes, attached at four points with screws to frame 1 of the fuselage that also worked as firewall. The engine was easy to dismount after taking off a three-piece duraluminum plate cowling with water drop shaped stampings over the valve tappets and unscrewing four bolts. It

Hs 123 A-1, yellow L from 4./SG 2 taxiing for take off from an air strip in Russia.

was very important in difficult conditions of the front line repair shops.

Fuel was mixed with air in the double-flow, twin-choke Pallas-Stromberg NAY-9A carburetor with a convector using exhaust from cylinders number 5 and 6. The heat was transferred via engine oil. The use of the convector was particularly important in the harsh conditions of the Russian winter.

The constant mixture flow to all nine cylinders was provided by a turbo blower powered by elastic coupling with gear-wheels at the end of the crankshaft. The boost pressure was about 1.30kg/cm³. The BMW 132A-3 engine used 87 octane fuel fed to the cylinders with a Ehrich & Graetz ZD 350 pump with the pressure of 0.25kg/cm³. There were four outlet manifolds with round exhaust pipes at the end.

Oil flow was forced by a pump activated by the engine. The pump provided average oil pressure of 6.4kg/cm³. The 48.7dm³ oil tank, that was installed in front of frame number 1, was usually filled with 40dm³ of oil. Below it, there was a 2.7dm³ radiator.

The engine was fitted with two Bosch Magnetzünder GE 9-BRS magnetos and the Bosch Schwungkraft-Anlasser Serie SKH 375/10 000 A R 1 starter.

The engine powered the twin-blade, right-handed twist, duraluminum Junkers Ju Pak Hornet propeller with a diameter of 3.10m. The propeller pitch could be adjusted on the ground. Electricity was provided by the Bosch LJ 600/24 AI 10 generator with the power of 600 Watt at 24 Volt. The electric installation powered the navigation lights, instrument lights, ignition devices and sparking plugs, pilot's suit heating system, reflex sight, radio and bomb release mechanism.

The Henschel 123 A-1 fuselage had an oval cross section and was entirely made of duraluminum. Its maximum height was 1,490mm and maximum width at the firewall was 1,055mm. The length of the fuselage, from the engine cradle attachment point to the rudder axis of rotation, was 6,145mm. The monocoque struc-

The Hs 123 A-1 aircraft from II./Schl.G 1 participated in the battle of Kursk in July 1943.

Rear view of the same aircraft.

installed at the leading edge in the middle of the upper wing. The antenna line was stretched between the antenna pole and the top of the vertical stabilizer.

The cockpit was between frames 4 and 5. It was made of metal plates and dowmetal tubes welded together, with duraluminum plates riveted to them. The pilot's seat, made of stamped metal plate, was adapted for the seat parachute. The height of the seat was adjustable within 113mm, which could also be done in flight, making the pilot's position comfortable. The aircraft was controlled with the KG II control stick and rudder pedals.

The main instrument panel was made of dowmetal painted with RLM 02 Grau. The instruments and switches were placed in two rows. Below, there was an auxiliary instrument panel which, apart from gauges, included radio operating switches and the instrument panel light dimmer. On both sides of the cockpit, there were doors for entering the aircraft. To make it easier for the pilot to enter the cockpit, two steps covered with flaps and straps were fitted to both sides of the fuselage. The full frames 9 and 10 in the rear section of the fuselage were used to attach the vertical and horizontal stabilizers. The single vertical stabilizer had metal structure, the rudder was controlled with steel cables and was fitted with a trimmer operated from the cockpit. The rudder, in the neutral position, was locked 2° left to compensate for the propeller torque.

The horizontal stabilizer was supported by single struts made of steel tubes with duraluminum fairing which made an oval cross section. The control surfaces of the Hs 123 A-1 were covered with fabric while the B-1 version had duraluminum covering. The structure of each horizontal stabilizer was based on six duraluminum ribs. The standard angle of setting was +3°. The elevators, fitted with trimmers, were controlled with pushers and steel cables. The horizontal stabilizer was attached to frames number 9a and 9b with four fork bolts.

The top wing had dual structure and rectangular contour with rounded tips. Its two parts were screwed together in the middle section and attached to the fuselage with metal struts. Two faired interwing struts connected the top wing with the lower wings. To give the pilot better visibility of the upper half-sphere, the middle section of the top wing had shorter ribbing and its skin presented a characteristic semicircular cut over the fuselage. Each of the top wing halves had duraluminum structure with two main spars, auxiliary spars and 21 ribs. The A-1 version had the upper section of the wing partially covered with fabric while the B-1 version had metal covering. The B-1 version was also fitted with a new type of attachment for

ture of the fuselage was covered by smooth duraluminum plates with rectangular panels for accessing the ammunition containers of both fuselage mounted machine guns. The fuselage constituted ten main and five auxiliary frames. The frames were stiffened by four main longerons and a dozen or so auxiliary ones in the rear section of the fuselage.

The 1 and 2 frames were also the firewalls. Between them, there was the main 270dm³ fuel tank fitted with a valve for emergency fuel dump. The lower wings were attached to frame 1 and 2, three brackets of the upper wing were attached to the upper part of each frame. Between frames 2a and 3, there were ammunition containers for the 7.92mm MG 17 machine guns, behind them, there was the Telefunken FuG VII short-wave radio working on 2,500 to 3,750kHz waveband. The 50cm antenna was aileron hinges at the end of ribs number 11, 15 and 19. The bottom part, except for the middle section, the surface between ribs 14 and 15 and the wing tips, was in both versions covered with fabric. The slotted ailerons were balanced, covered with fabric and controlled with pushers. Above the fuselage, on the top wing, there was the antenna mast attachment point where a 50cm long, wooden mast was fitted with thumbscrews. The wing tips were fitted with navigation lights with 20 Watt bulbs. The lights were covered with red glass shade on the left wing and green on the right.

The two-section bottom wing had one spar and 13 ribs in each section. The wings were attached with screws to the fuselage frames 1 and 2 at three points. The attachment point was covered with metal fairing. Counting from the centre line of the fuselage, the leading edge of the bottom wing was receded 39.2cm in relation to the top wing's leading edge. Similarly to the top wing, the upper part of the bottom wing was mostly covered with fabric in the A-1 version, the B-1 had the whole surface covered with duraluminum. In the lower part, between ribs number 2 and 4, there were slotted landing flaps with their control mechanism installed along the main wing spar. Electrical wires of the bomb release system and the speedometer pipes were placed inside aluminum tubes. Ribs number 0 of both lower wings had attachment points for additional, external aluminum fuel tank with 130dm³ capacity. The tank could be jettisoned in the air.

The fixed undercarriage consisted of two independent one-leg units covered with dowmetal fairing that made the undercarriage leg cover and two-part wheel cover. The individual parts were connected with clasp locks. The fairing reached 10cm below the wheel axle. In the field conditions of the Eastern Front, during winter, autumn and spring, the fairings were removed as snow and mud that got stuck between the fairing and the tyre would block the wheel. The main undercarriage wheel track was 2,342mm. The undercarriage legs and the rear struts with the fork were made of steel and duraluminum tubes that were fitted to the bottom wing. The legs had spring shock absorption. The wheels were dowmetal cast produced by the Elektron company in Cannstatt. They were fitted with drum brakes activated independently with pedals. The 690x200mm tyres were produced by the Continental company in Stuttgart. Their internal pressure was 2.6 atmosphere. The one-legged tail wheel, the Elektron-Spornrad R 1802 made by the Elektron company or the B-3503 B made by the Kronprinz in Solingen, was attached to frame number 9. Both types were adapted for the 290x110mm Continental tyres with 3.25 atmosphere internal pressure. The tail

undercarriage leg with the fork had hydraulic shock absorption.

The Henschel Hs 123 A-1 had fixed armament consisting of the So 1-17 device that operated the two synchronized Rheinmetall-Borsig MG 17, 7.92mm machine guns. The machine guns, mounted in the front upper section of the fuselage, fired between the engine's cylinders and through special openings in the cowling. 500 rounds of ammunition for each gun were stored in boxes placed in the fuselage. Pneumatic installation was used to cock and re-cock the guns. The system was fitted with the Revi IIIb reflex sight mounted above the main section of the instrument panel in a cut-out in the armoured windshield. The Hs 123 V6 had two additional MG 17, 7.92mm machine guns with 500 rounds of ammunition per gun, mounted in pods under the bottom wings.

The attack armament was operated by the So III installation. It consisted of four single ETC 50/VIIIb bomb carriers mounted in pairs under the lower wings. The racks could carry four SC 50 type, 50kg bombs (SC = Sprengbombe Cylindrisch – cylindrical fragmentation bomb). Alternatively, the SD 50 bombs could be used (SD = Sprengbombe Dickwandig – thick-wall fragmentation bomb). Additionally, the tube containers in the fuselage could carry ten 10kg SC 10 or SD 10 A bombs. The use of this weapon system, designated So II-Anlage, in production aircraft is not documented.

The Spanish air force used 70kg bombs. They could be fitted with one-metre rods with contact fuses mounted in the front part of the bomb. The bombs would explode above the ground thus enlarging their kill zone. For the fist time the system called Santiago Mendi was used during the Spanish Civil War. The German variant, known as Dinort-Stäbe (Dinort's sticks), was widely used on the Eastern Front.

Paint schemes and markings of the Henschel Hs 123 in the Luftwaffe service

The Henschel 123 V1, V2 and V3 prototypes probably had all surfaces painted with RLM 63 Grau and the Hs 123 V4, V5, V6 and V7 prototypes were painted with RLM 02 Grau. The prototype aircraft had civilian letter registration

Henschel Hs 123 A-1 specifications	
Power plant	BMW 132A-3 nine-cylinder, radial engine with maximum power of 632hp (465 kW)
Wingspan	top wing – 10.5 m
	bottom wing – 8.0 m
Length	8.33 m
Height	3.21 m
Wing area	total – 24.85 m²
	top wing – 16.24 m²
	bottom wing – 8.61 m²
Propeller diameter	2.9 m
Empty weight	1,420 kg
Take off weight	2,175 kg
Wing loading	87.4kg/m²
Power loading	3.3 kg/hp
Maximum speed at altitude:	0m – 285 km/h
	2,400m – 290 km/h
	4,000m – 278 km/h
	5,000m – 265 km/h
	7,000m – 240 km/h
Diving speed	55 km/h
Cruising speed at 2,000m	260 km/h
Landing speed	100–105 km/h
Service ceiling	6,100 m
Rate of climb to altitude:	2,400 m – 4 min 24 sec
	4,000 m – 12 min 10 sec
	5,000 m – 19 min 8 sec
	6,000 m – 36 min 24 sec
Range:	at ground level with 100 kg external load – 500 km
	at ground level with 200 kg external load – 325 km
	at 4,000m with 100 kg external load – 750 km
	at 4,000m with 200 kg external load – 480 km
Armament:	Two fixed MG 17, 7.92 mm machine guns with 500 rounds of ammunition per gun.
	External bomb load of 450 kg.

starting with the letters D-I..., where D stood for the name of the country (Deutschland) and I was the code letter for military aircraft of B1 class – with weight between 1,000 and 2,500kg and crew of 1 to 4. The Hs V1, V2 and V3 had a red stripe with white circle and a swastika on the left side of their vertical stabilizers and on the right – horizontal stripe with national colours, from the top: black, white and red. In accordance with regulation No. 78 from 29 August 1936, the three-colour stripe on the right side of the stabilizer was replaced with a red stripe with white circle and a black swastika. Regulation No. 5 from 30 January 1939 changed the scheme to black swastika with white edging and thin black framing on both sides of the stabilizer. The production aircraft were initially painted according to a scheme introduced in the Luftwaffe at the turn of 1936 and 1937 – RLM 65 Hellblau on the bottom surfaces and three colour (RLM 61 Braun, RLM 62 Grün and RLM 63 Grau) angular camouflage patches on the upper and side surfaces. Two standard schemes for camouflage patches layout were used, called variant A and B.

Since 1938, in accordance with the Entwurf L.Dv. 521/1 document, a new painting scheme for land aircraft was introduced. It included RLM 65 Hellblau on bottom surfaces of the airframe and angular camouflage patches in RLM 70 Schwarzgrün amd RLM 71 Dunkelgrün on the upper and side surfaces.

However, photographic documentation proves that the aircraft produced before 1938 had the three-colour camouflage on their upper and side surfaces. The Hs 123 with that paint scheme participated in the campaigns against Poland and France. More aircraft with the camouflage in two shades of green did not appear until the Balkan campaign in spring of 1941. The winter camouflage on the Eastern Front was made by covering the upper and side surfaces with lime or easy-to-wash white paint. The white colour was usually applied unevenly so the standard green camouflage could be seen underneath.

As national markings, the aircraft had straight-armed crosses (Balkenkreuz) on both sides of the top wing and the fuselage and a swastika (Hakenkreuz) on both sides of the vertical stabilizer.

During the Balkan campaign in spring of 1941, quick identification markings were introduced by painting the engine cowling and rudder with RLM 04 Gelb. On the Eastern Front, the bottom parts of the upper wing tips and a stripe of different width in the rear section of the fuselage were painted with RLM 04 Gelb. Before the war, the aircraft of St.G 162 and 165 had standard five-symbol unit markings on the sides of the fuselage. The first symbol of the fuselage code defined the air district (Luft-kreis), the second was the number of air regiment (Geschwader), the third was an individual designation of the aircraft, the fourth marked a squadron (Gruppe), the fifth – a flight (Staffel), e.g. 52+B13 is the B aircraft from 3.Staffel, I Gruppe, St.G 165.

Later, when II.(Schl.)/LG 2 was equipped with the Hs 123, the unit markings were painted on the fuselages e.g. L2+HN = L2 – Lehrgeschwader 2 designation, H individual letter of the aircraft in the flight colours (white for 4. Staffel, red for 5. Staffel or yellow for 6. Staffel), N – 5. Staffel designation.

In Schlachtgeschwader 1, the Hs 123 had markings typical for attack units painted on the fuselages, geometric markings designating executive aircraft of Stab swarms, black triangles and letter designations in colours of particular flights.

Training units, apart from coloured letters in front of the cockpit, also used yellow of white number markings.

Most aircraft used by SG 1 had the Infantry Assault Badge (Infanterie-Sturmabzeichen) painted with white colour on the fuselage, behind the engine cowling. Sometimes, the unit's emblem was painted near the cockpit. Some aircraft were marked with pilots' personal insignia e.g. the attack aircraft ace, Hptm. Josef Menapace had his friend's name (Rolf von Zahradnicek) painted on the fuselage, Zahradnicek was killed during a combat mission over Russia.

Bibliography

Bekker Cajus: Angriffshöhe 4000, Oldenburg 1964.

Cull Brian, Lander Bruce, *Weiss Heinrich: Twelve days in May*, London 1995.

Emmerling Marius: *Luftwaffe nad Polską 1939, część III: Stukaflieger*, Gdynia 2006.

Galland Adolf: *Die Ersten und die Letzten*, Darmstadt 1984.

Höfling Rudolf: *Henschel Hs 123, die Geschichte eines legendären Schlachtflugzeuges*, Stengelheim 2005.

Strohmeyer Curt: *Stukas*, Berlin 1941.

Endnotes

1 Mordawski Hubert: *Siły powietrzne w I wojnie światowej*, Wrocław 2008, p. 251.

2 Ibidem, p. 310.

3 Ibidem, p. 430.

4 Ernst Udet (1896-1941) achieved 62 aerial victories and, after Manfred von Richthofen, was the second scoring ace of the German fighter air force during World War I. He was the chief of the Technical Department and then the General Armourer responsible for aviation equipment supplies. What is interesting is the fact that on 8 May 1935 Ernst Udet was still a civilian and did not join the reborn Luftwaffe until 1 June 1935, in the rank of Oberst. (author's remark)

5 Robert Ritter von Greim (1892-1945) scored 26 victories during the World War I. The last Luftwaffe commander, appointed by Hitler on 23 April 1945 after Göring's dismissal. (author's remark)

6 Oscar Dinort (1901-1965) one of the best known Stuka aces, recipient of the Knight's Cross with Oak Leaves, from October 1939 to October 1941 the commanding officer of St.G 2 Immelmann then worked as a staff officer. (author's remark)

7 One of the prototypes was fitted with the Revi C/12A sight. (author's remark)

8 The Fliegerführer z.b.V's combat diary recorded the following von Richthofen's statement: "Before Spielvogel and his crows reach the Polish border from Altsiedel, they will have used half of their fuel."

9 Blumenkrieg – the name given by the Germans to the operation of annexation of Austria where the Wehrmacht troops were greeted with flowers. (author's remark)

10 These were the advance troops of the 27 Infantry Regiment. (author's remark)

11 Bekker Cajus: Angriffshöhe 4000, Oldenburg 1964, p. 21-22.

12 Detailed information concerning actions of II.(Schl.)/LG 2 in the September campaign of 1939 are presented according to the book by Emmerling Marius: Luftwaffe nad Polską 1939, part III Stukaflieger, Gdynia 2006. (author's remark)

13 It can be translated as "an acoustic wave affecting the head" (author's remark)

14 Höfling Rudolf: Henschel Hs 123, die Geschichte eines legendären Schlachtflugzeuges, Stengelheim 2005, p. 20.

15 Strohmeyer Curt: Stukas! Erlebnis eines Fliegerkorps, Berlin 1941, p. 123-127.

16 Emmerling Marius: *Luftwaffe nad Polską 1939, część III: Stukaflieger*, Gdynia 2006, p. 111-112.

17 Strohmeyer Curt: Stukas, Berlin 1941, p. 25-27.

18 Galland Adolf: *Die Ersten und die Letzten*, Darmstadt 1984, p. 44.

19 The Hurricane pilot, Flt. Lt. John Sullivan from 242 Squadron was killed, see Cull Brian, Lander Bruce i Weiss Heinrich: Twelve days in May, London 1995, p. 118

20 Georg Dörffer later became one of the greatest Luftwaffe attack aircraft aces, he flew 1004 combat missions and scored 30 aerial victories, appointed commander of SG 4, died in Italy on 26.05.1944. Recipient of the Knight's Cross with Oak Leaves on 14.04.1943. (author's remark)

21 Interesting is the fact that Werner Mölders received the Knight's Cross as the first Luftwaffe fighter pilot as late as 29.05.1940! (author's remark)

22 Höfling Rudolf..., op. cit., p. 30.

23 Strohmeyer..., op. cit., p. 186-190.

24 Ibidem, p. 273-276.

25 Ibidem, p. 276.

26 Höfling Rudolf..., op. cit., p. 33.

27 Capitán – Captain, Teniente – Lieutenant, Alférez – Second Lieutenant. (author's remark)

28 As a comparison, the price of one Messerschmitt Bf 109 E-3 was at that time 102,489.36RM and dropped in November 1940 to 68,622.54RM. The average price of one Bf 109 E, estimated after its production ended, was about 86,000RM. (author's remark)

29 Dive bomber squadron. (author's remark)

30 Spanish Air Force. (author's remark)

31 Almost twice as high as the Hs 123 A sold to Spain in 1939. (author's remark)

32 German Trade Company for industrial products. (author's remark)

33 Some sources say, the top and side surfaces were first painted with sand colour and the snake-shaped lines were added later. Due to poor quality of available photographs, this dispute remains unsettled. (author's remark)

34 Air Regiment Nr 2. (author's remark)

35 Literally „Grabenkampf", meaning to fight "in trenches" (author's remark)

36 Schalk was mistaken as the Hs 123 could carry up to 450kg of bombs. (author's remark)

37 Independent Fighter Bomber Squadron. (author's remark)

Messerschmitt Me 262
Schwalbe vol. I, II

- **3D colour visualisations of construction details**
- **dozens of photos**
- **design and development**
- **production and experimental variants**
- **operational history**
- **camouflage and markings**

MONOGRAPHS · 3D EDITION

46

Marek J. Murawski
Marek Ryś

Messerschmitt
Me 262
Schwalbe

KAGERO

MONOGRAPHS · 3D EDITION

47

Marek J. Murawski
Marek Ryś

Messerschmitt
Me 262
Schwalbe
vol. II

KAGERO

www.kagero.p

MONOGRAFIE MONOGRAPHS

Henschel Hs 123

Opracował i rysował: © Mariusz Łukasik 2012

The drawings have been prepared using previously published literature, documentary evidence
and contemporary photographs, as well as photographs of museum examples
Rysunki zostały opracowane na podstawie podanej literatury,
zdjęć dokumentalnych oraz zdjęć egzemplarzy muzealnych.

KAGERO
1:48 Scale
© Mariusz Łukasik 2012

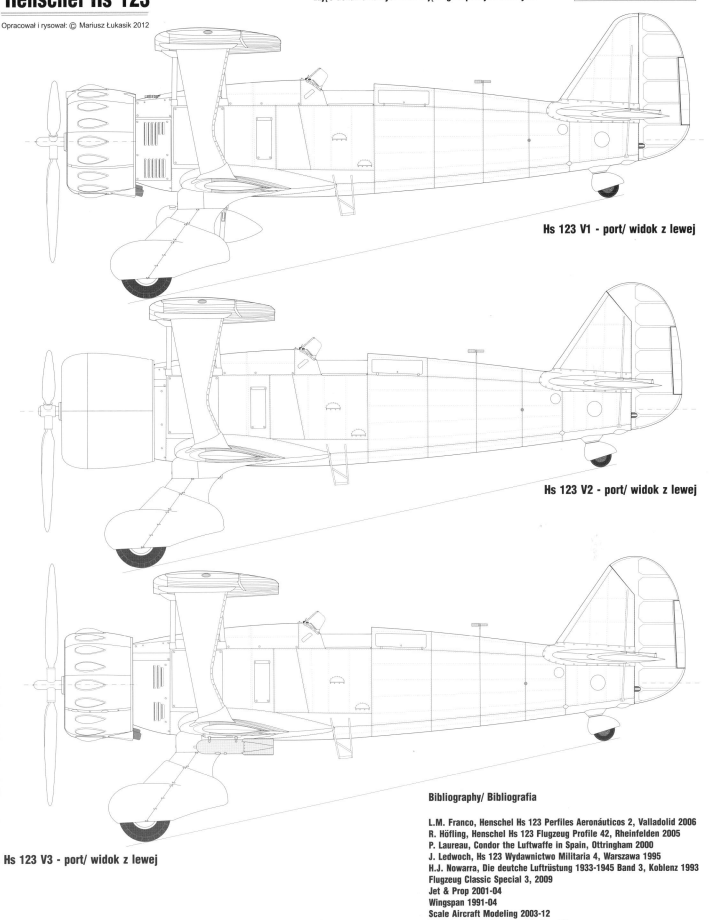

Hs 123 V1 - port/ widok z lewej

Hs 123 V2 - port/ widok z lewej

Hs 123 V3 - port/ widok z lewej

Bibliography/ Bibliografia

L.M. Franco, Henschel Hs 123 Perfiles Aeronáuticos 2, Valladolid 2006
R. Höfling, Henschel Hs 123 Flugzeug Profile 42, Rheinfelden 2005
P. Laureau, Condor the Luftwaffe in Spain, Ottringham 2000
J. Ledwoch, Hs 123 Wydawnictwo Militaria 4, Warszawa 1995
H.J. Nowarra, Die deutsche Luftrüstung 1933-1945 Band 3, Koblenz 1993
Flugzeug Classic Special 3, 2009
Jet & Prop 2001-04
Wingspan 1991-04
Scale Aircraft Modeling 2003-12
Luftfahrt International Bande 2 und 3
L.Dv. 383, Hs 123 A und B Flugzeug-Handbuch, 1938
L.Dv. 384, Hs 123 A und B Flugzeug-Beschreibung, 1937

Attention! In some views the course of riveted joints have been simplified for the drawings clearness
Uwaga! Na części rzutów uproszczono dla czytelności rysunku przebieg szwów nitowych

0   0,5   1   2   3m

MONOGRAFIE MONOGRAPHS

Henschel Hs 123

Opracował i rysował: © Mariusz Łukasik 2012

KAGERO
1:48 Scale
©Mariusz Łukasik 2012

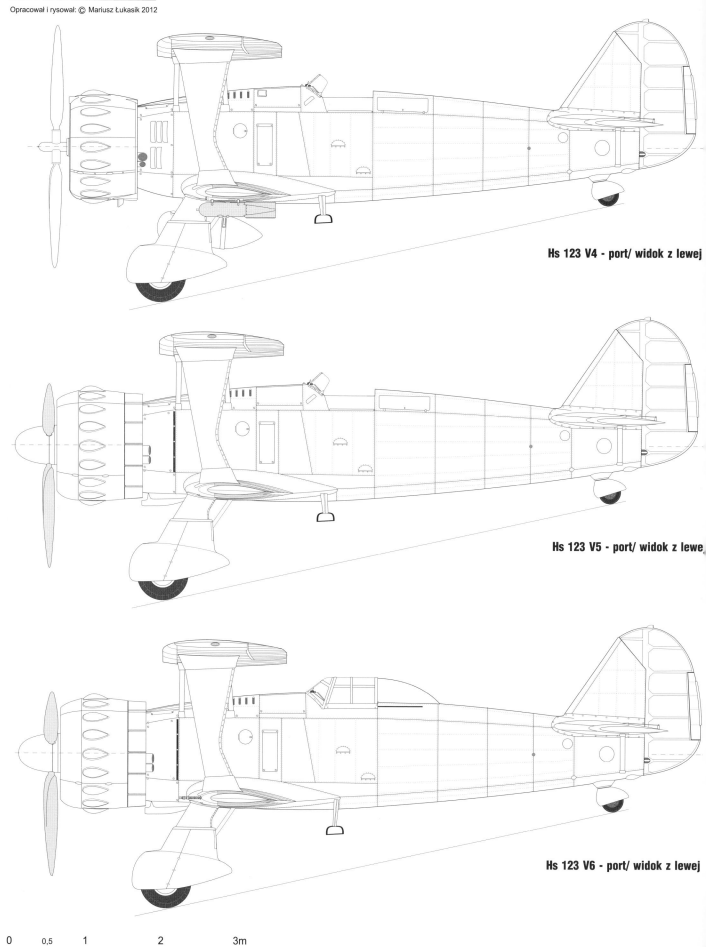

Hs 123 V4 - port/ widok z lewej

Hs 123 V5 - port/ widok z lewe

Hs 123 V6 - port/ widok z lewej

0   0,5   1   2   3m

KAGERO
1:48 Scale
© Mariusz Łukasik 2012

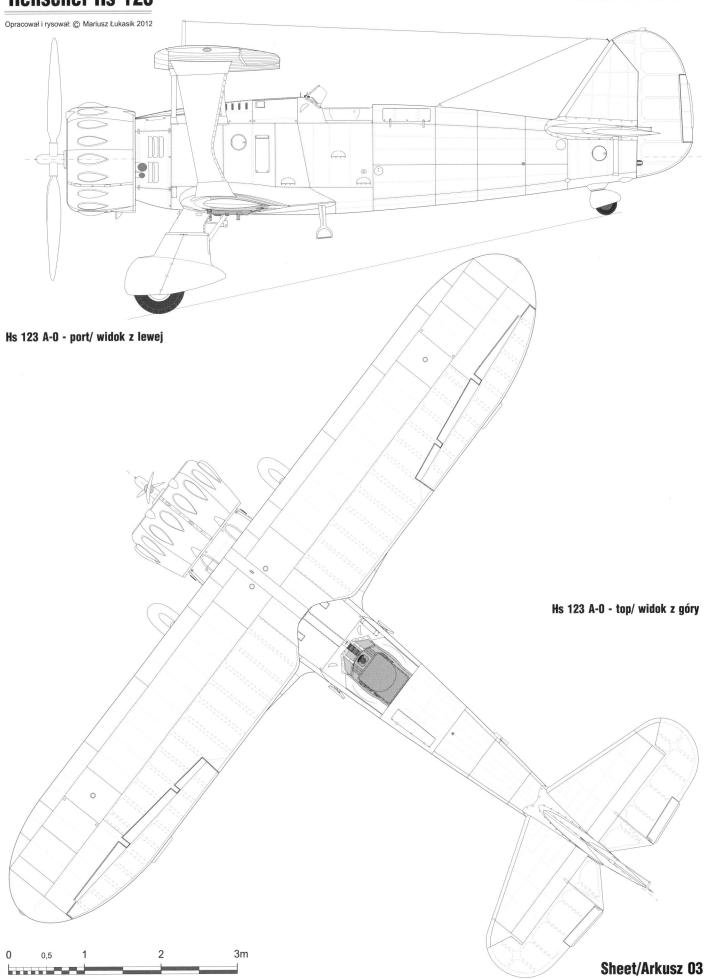

Hs 123 A-0 - port/ widok z lewej

Hs 123 A-0 - top/ widok z góry

0   0,5   1   2   3m

Sheet/Arkusz 03

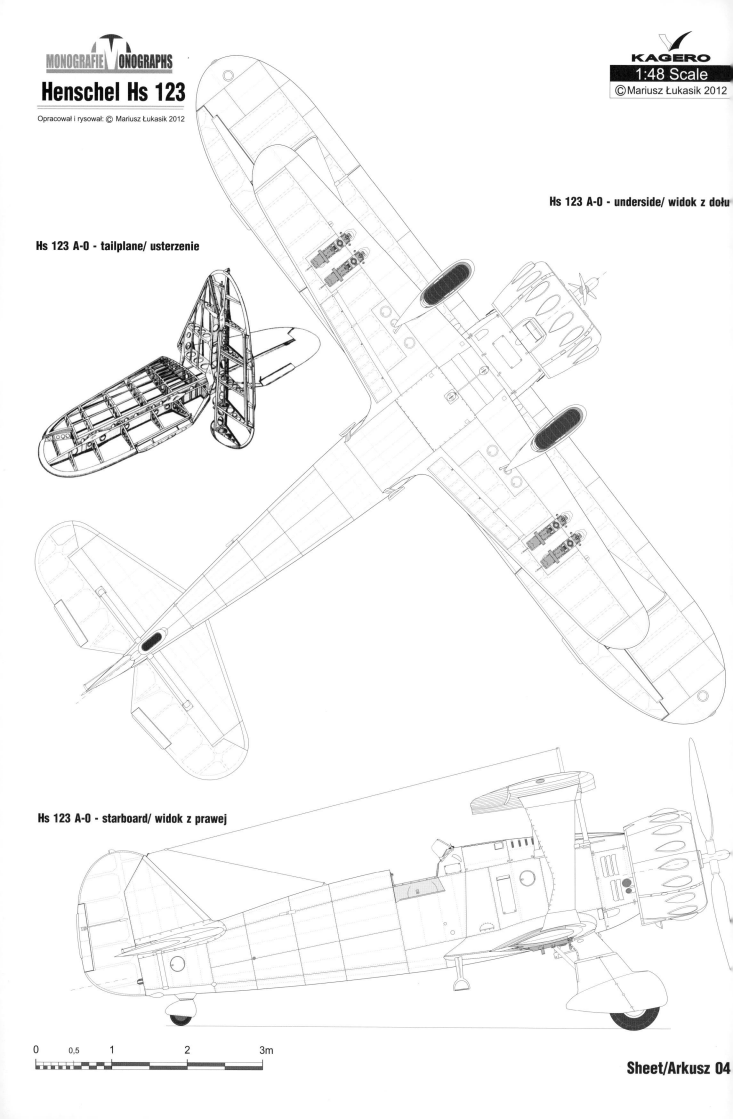

MONOGRAFIE MONOGRAPHS

Henschel Hs 123

Opracował i rysował: © Mariusz Łukasik 2012

KAGERO
1:48 Scale
© Mariusz Łukasik 2012

Hs 123 A-0 - underside/ widok z dołu

Hs 123 A-0 - tailplane/ usterzenie

Hs 123 A-0 - starboard/ widok z prawej

0   0,5   1   2   3m

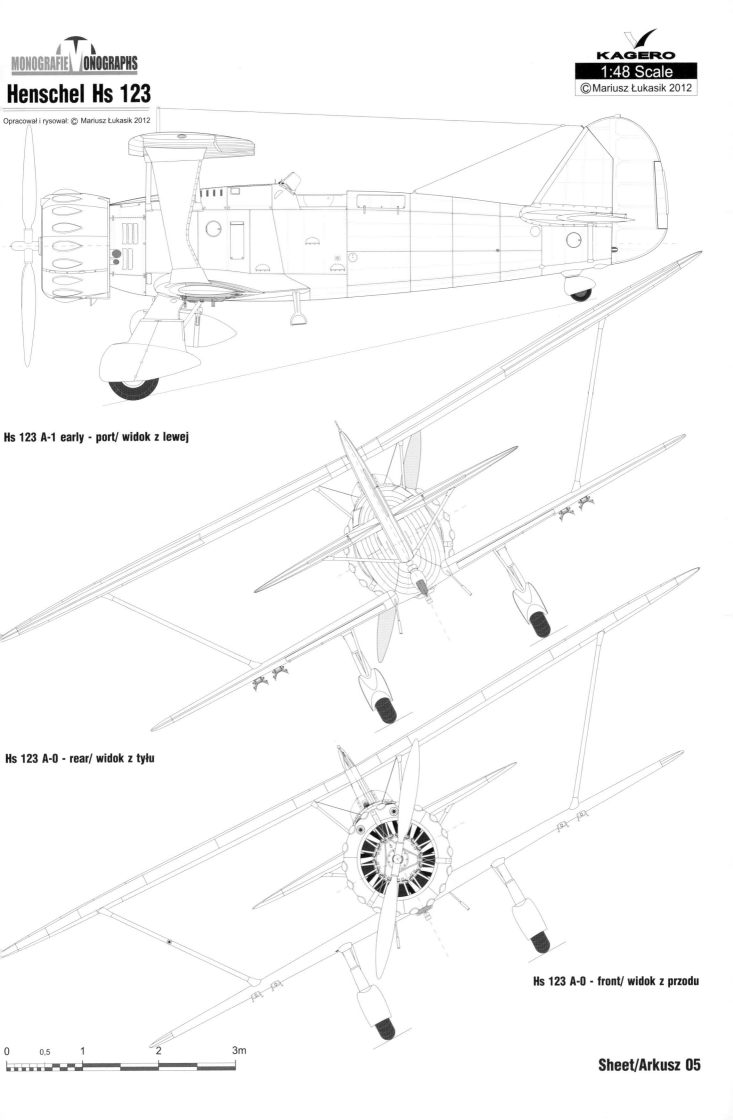

MONOGRAFIE MONOGRAPHS

Henschel Hs 123

Opracował i rysował: © Mariusz Łukasik 2012

KAGERO
1:48 Scale
© Mariusz Łukasik 2012

Hs 123 A-1 early - port/ widok z lewej

Hs 123 A-0 - rear/ widok z tyłu

Hs 123 A-0 - front/ widok z przodu

0   0,5   1   2   3m

Sheet/Arkusz 05

Henschel Hs 123

Opracował i rysował: © Mariusz Łukasik 2012

1:48 Scale
© Mariusz Łukasik 2012

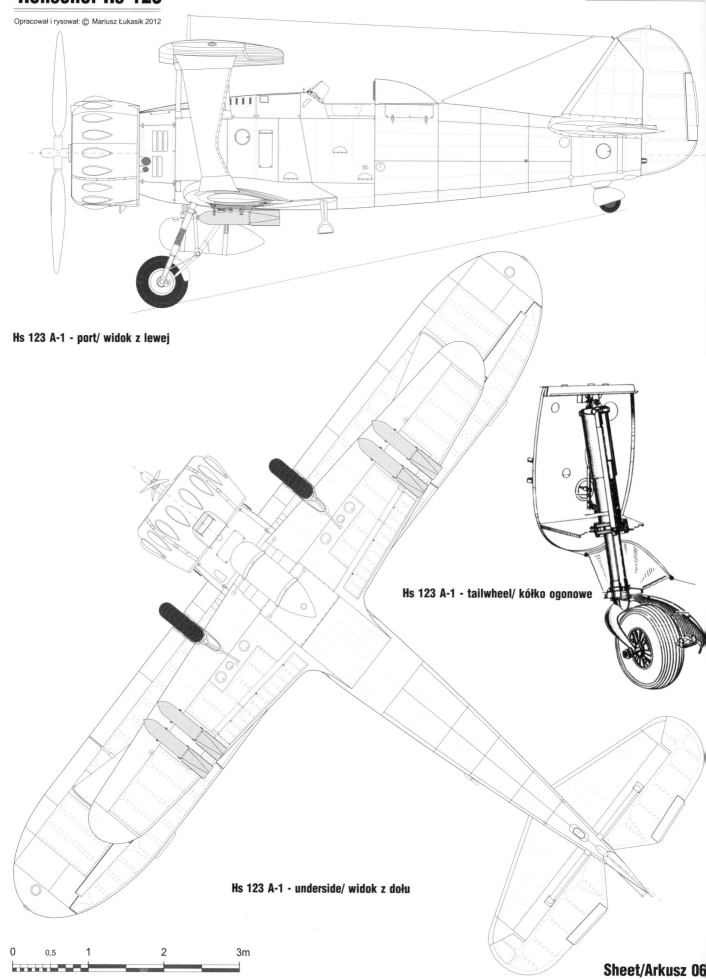

Hs 123 A-1 - port/ widok z lewej

Hs 123 A-1 - tailwheel/ kółko ogonowe

Hs 123 A-1 - underside/ widok z dołu

0   0,5   1   2   3m

Sheet/Arkusz 06

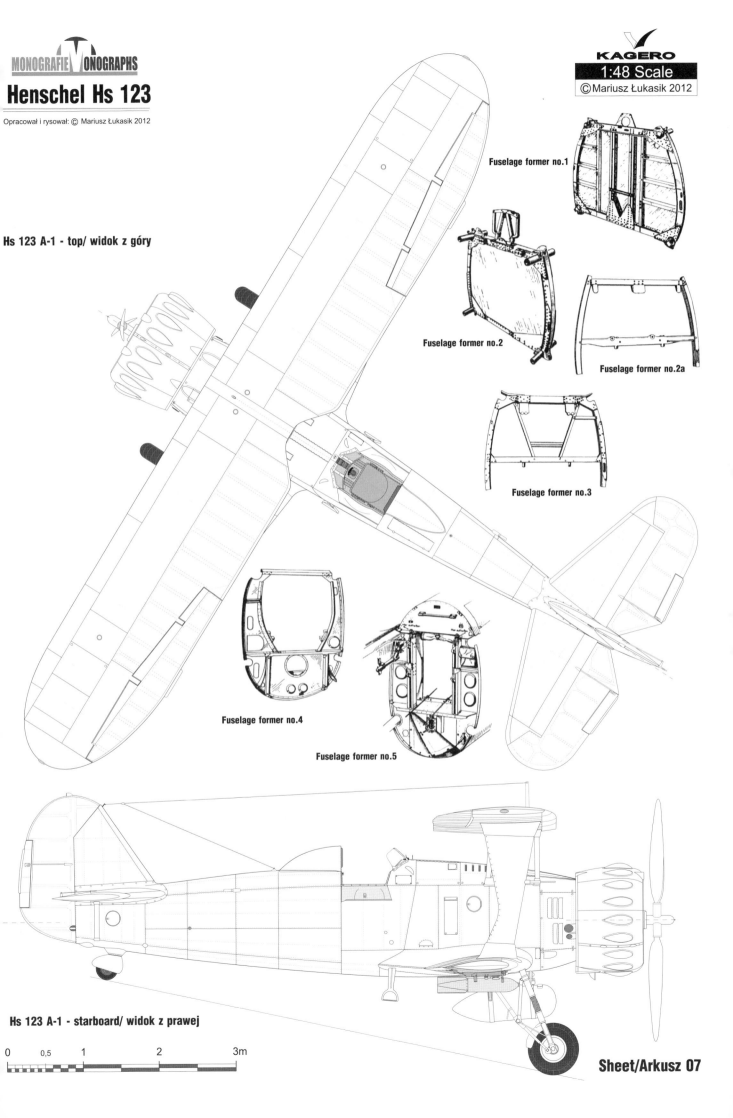

MONOGRAFIE MONOGRAPHS

Henschel Hs 123

Opracował i rysował: © Mariusz Łukasik 2012

KAGERO
1:48 Scale
©Mariusz Łukasik 2012

Fuselage former no.1

Hs 123 A-1 - top/ widok z góry

Fuselage former no.2

Fuselage former no.2a

Fuselage former no.3

Fuselage former no.4

Fuselage former no.5

Hs 123 A-1 - starboard/ widok z prawej

0   0,5   1   2   3m

Sheet/Arkusz 07

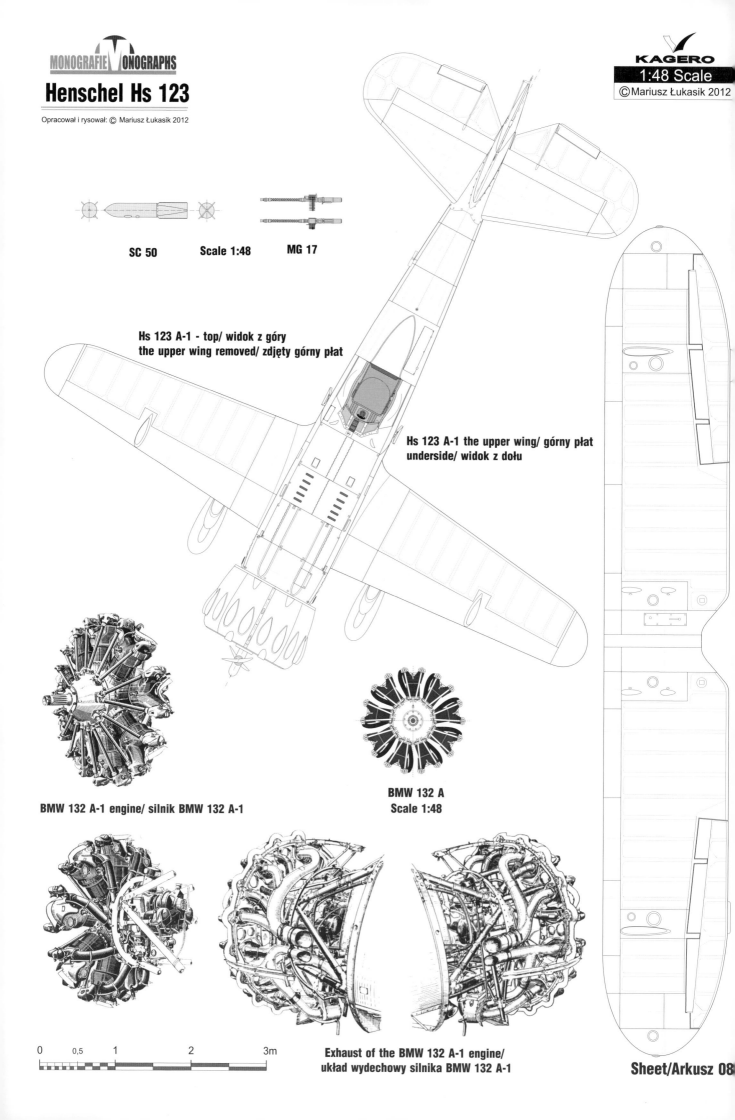

MONOGRAFIE MONOGRAPHS
Henschel Hs 123
Opracował i rysował: © Mariusz Łukasik 2012

KAGERO
1:48 Scale
© Mariusz Łukasik 2012

SC 50   **Scale 1:48**   **MG 17**

Hs 123 A-1 - top/ widok z góry
the upper wing removed/ zdjęty górny płat

Hs 123 A-1 the upper wing/ górny płat
underside/ widok z dołu

BMW 132 A-1 engine/ silnik BMW 132 A-1

BMW 132 A
Scale 1:48

Exhaust of the BMW 132 A-1 engine/
układ wydechowy silnika BMW 132 A-1

0   0,5   1   2   3m

Sheet/Arkusz 08

MONOGRAFIE MONOGRAPHS

Henschel Hs 123

Opracował i rysował: © Mariusz Łukasik 2012

KAGERO
1:48 Scale
© Mariusz Łukasik 2012

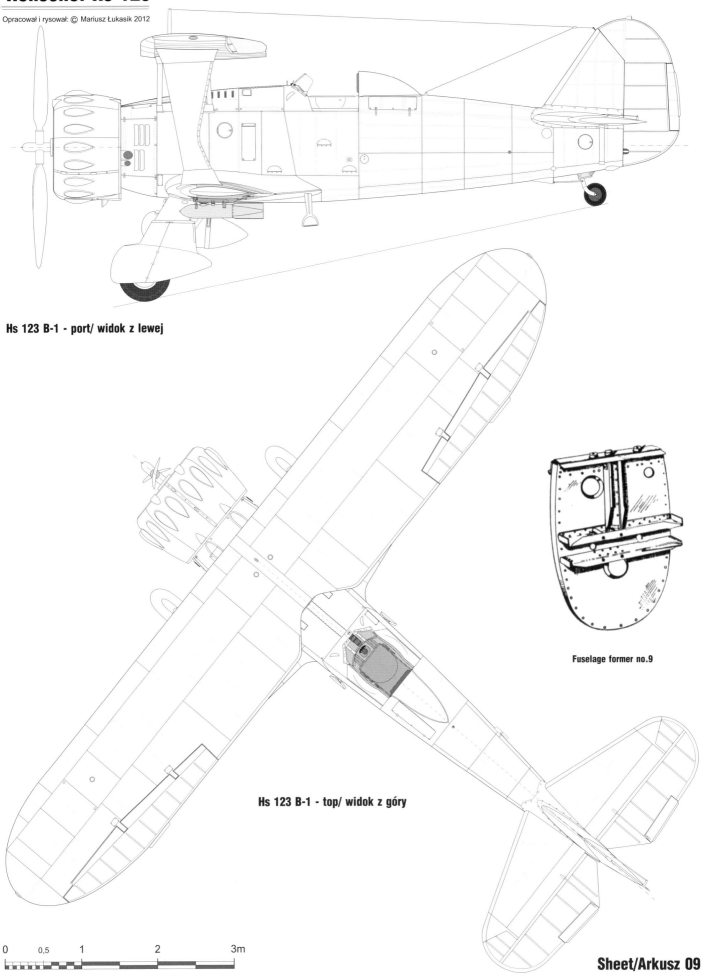

Hs 123 B-1 - port/ widok z lewej

Hs 123 B-1 - top/ widok z góry

Fuselage former no.9

0   0,5   1   2   3m

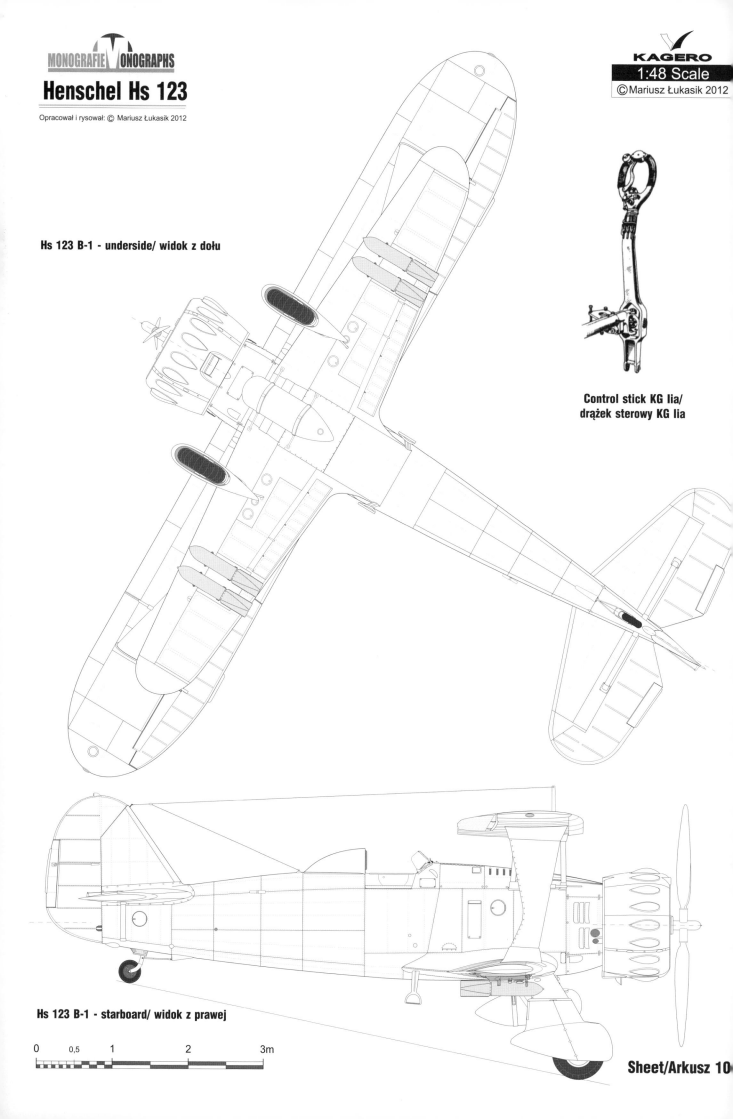

MONOGRAFIE MONOGRAPHS

Henschel Hs 123

Opracował i rysował: © Mariusz Łukasik 2012

KAGERO
1:48 Scale
©Mariusz Łukasik 2012

Hs 123 B-1 - underside/ widok z dołu

**Control stick KG IIa/
drążek sterowy KG IIa**

Hs 123 B-1 - starboard/ widok z prawej

0   0,5   1   2   3m

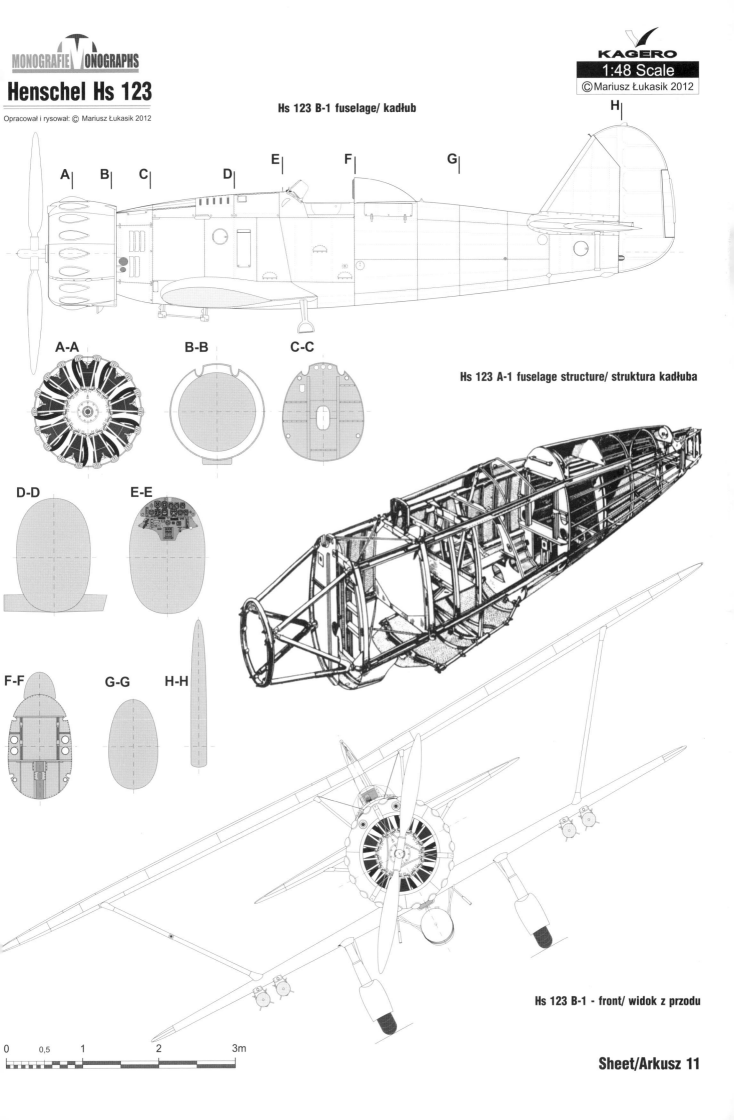

MONOGRAFIE MONOGRAPHS

Henschel Hs 123

Opracował i rysował: © Mariusz Łukasik 2012

KAGERO
1:48 Scale
© Mariusz Łukasik 2012

Hs 123 B-1 fuselage/ kadłub

A   B   C   D   E   F   G   H

A-A   B-B   C-C

Hs 123 A-1 fuselage structure/ struktura kadłuba

D-D   E-E

F-F   G-G   H-H

Hs 123 B-1 - front/ widok z przodu

0   0,5   1   2   3m

Sheet/Arkusz 11

Hs 123 A-0

MONOGRAFIE MONOGRAPHS
Henschel Hs 123

Opracował i rysował: © Mariusz Łukasik 2012

0   0,5   1   2   3m

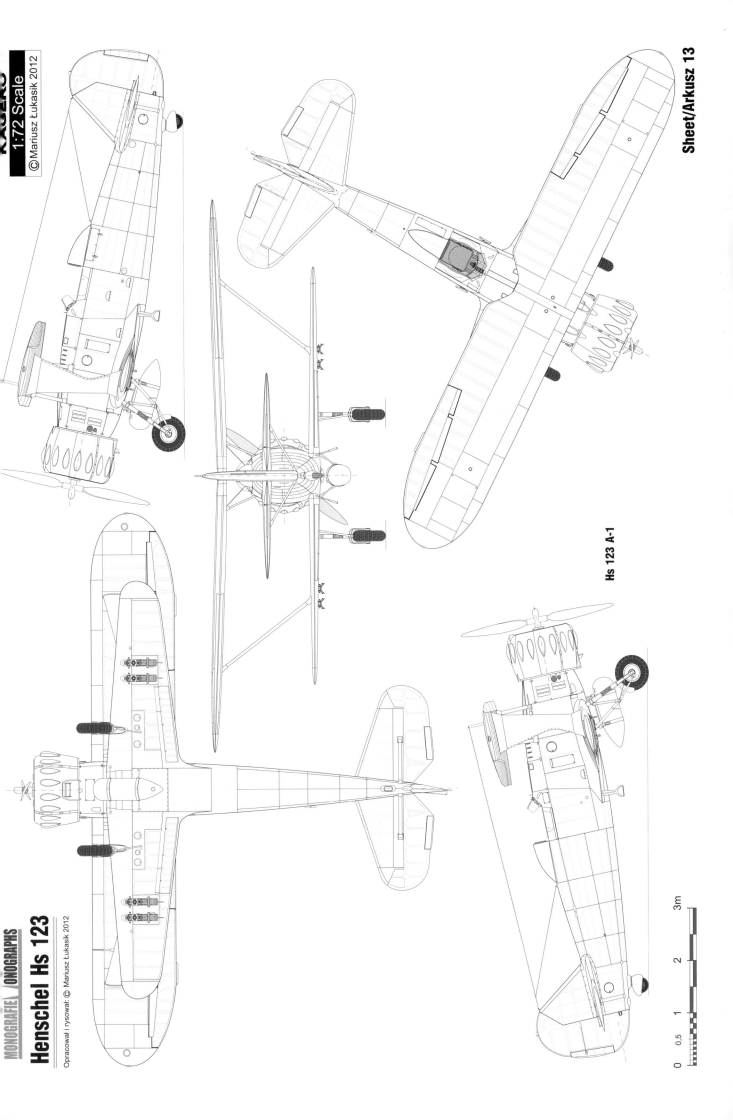

1:72 Scale

Sheet/Arkusz 13

Hs 123 A-1

MONOGRAFIE / MONOGRAPHS

Henschel Hs 123

Opracował i rysował: © Mariusz Łukasik 2012

0   0,5   1   2   3m

Hs 123 B-1

KAGERO
1:72 Scale
© Mariusz Łukasik 2012

MONOGRAFIE / MONOGRAPHS
Henschel Hs 123

Opracował i rysował: © Mariusz Łukasik 2012

0   0.5   1   2   3m

MONOGRAFIE / ONOGRAPHS

Henschel Hs 123

Opracował i rysował: © Mariusz Łukasik 2012

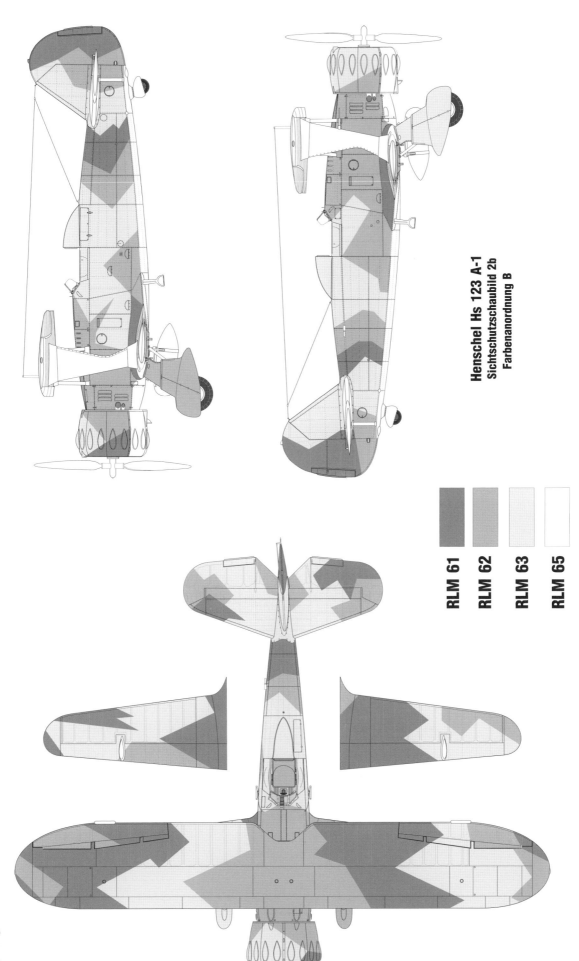

Henschel Hs 123 A-1
Sichtschutzschaubild 2b
Farbenanordnung B

RLM 61
RLM 62
RLM 63
RLM 65

0   0,5   1   2   3m

MONOGRAFIE MONOGRAPHS

Henschel Hs 123

Opracował i rysował: © Mariusz Łukasik 2012

KAGERO
1:72 Scale
© Mariusz Łukasik 2012

Specification of external changes
Wykaz zmian zewnętrznych w wersjach samolotu

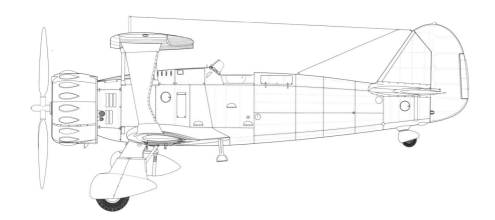

Hs 123 A-0

- first production version/
    pierwsza wersja produkcyjna

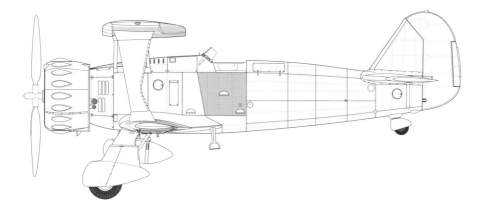

**Hs 123 A-1 early/wczesny
Spanish/ hiszpański**

- armoured cockpit sides/ opancerzenie boków kabiny
- lack of radio equipment/ brak instalacji radiowej

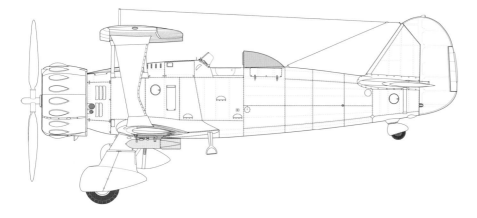

Hs 123 A-1

- turtle deck/ kozioł przeciwkapotażowy
- armoured cockpit/ opancerzenie kabiny

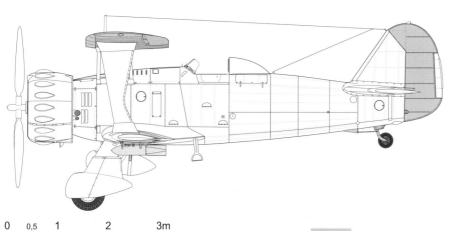

Hs 123 B-1

- metal skinned wings and control surfaces/
    skrzydła i stery kryte blachą
- modified tailplane/
    zmodyfikowane usterzenie poziome
- modified tailwheel/
    zmodyfikowane kółko ogonowe

0   0,5   1   2   3m

Zmiany / changes

Sheet/Arkusz 16

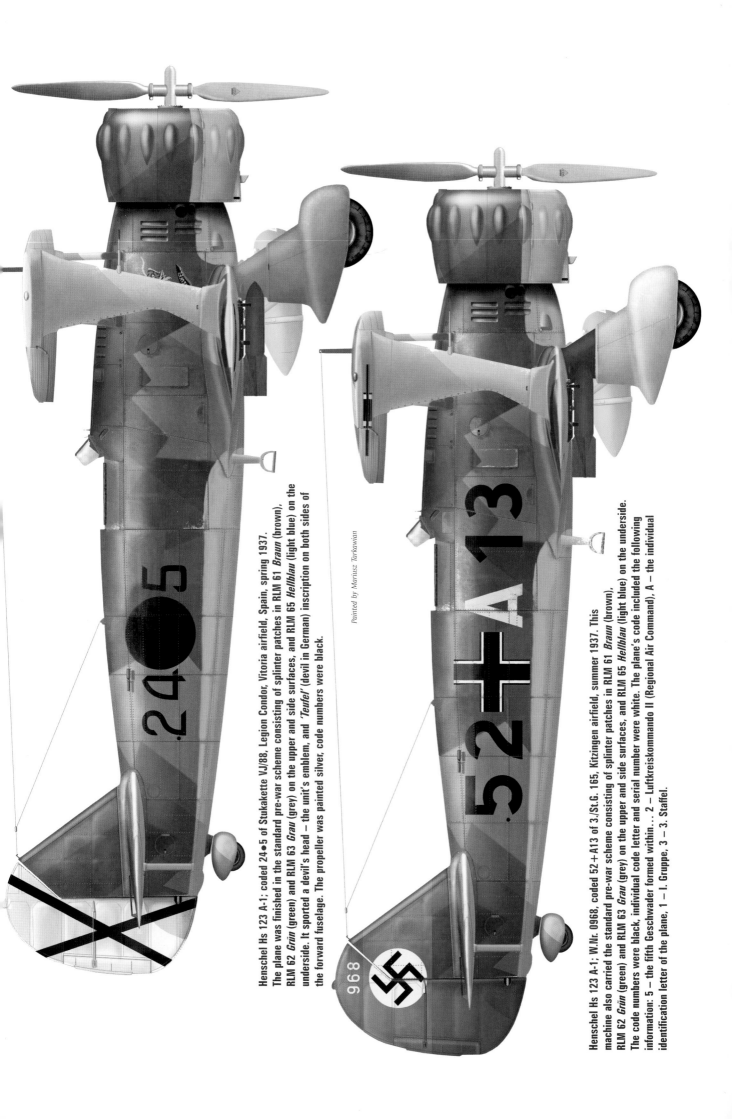

Henschel Hs 123 A-1; coded 24●5 of Stukakette VJ/88, Legion Condor, Vitoria airfield, Spain, spring 1937.
The plane was finished in the standard pre-war scheme consisting of splinter patches in RLM 61 *Braun* (brown),
RLM 62 *Grün* (green) and RLM 63 *Grau* (grey) on the upper and side surfaces, and RLM 65 *Hellblau* (light blue) on the
underside. It sported a devil's head – the unit's emblem, and *'Teufel'* (devil in German) inscription on both sides of
the forward fuselage. The propeller was painted silver, code numbers were black.

Painted by Mariusz Turkawian

Henschel Hs 123 A-1; W.Nr. 0968, coded 52+A13 of 3./St.G. 165, Kitzingen airfield, summer 1937. This
machine also carried the standard pre-war scheme consisting of splinter patches in RLM 61 *Braun* (brown),
RLM 62 *Grün* (green) and RLM 63 *Grau* (grey) on the upper and side surfaces, and RLM 65 *Hellblau* (light blue) on the underside.
The code numbers were black, individual code letter and serial number were white. The plane's code included the following
information: 5 – the fifth Geschwader formed within... 2 – Luftkreiskommando II (Regional Air Command), A – the individual
identification letter of the plane, 1 – I. Gruppe, 3 – 3. Staffel.

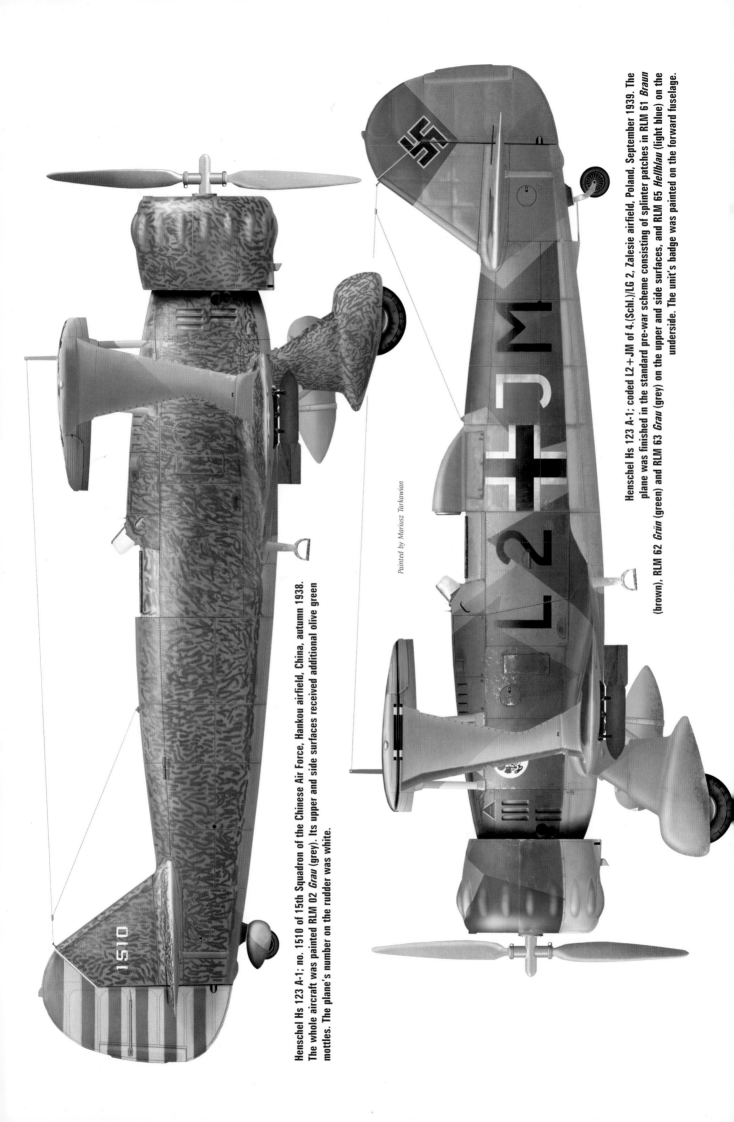

Henschel Hs 123 A-1; no. 1510 of 15th Squadron of the Chinese Air Force, Hankou airfield, China, autumn 1938. The whole aircraft was painted RLM 02 *Grau* (grey). Its upper and side surfaces received additional olive green mottles. The plane's number on the rudder was white.

Painted by Mariusz Tarkawian

Henschel Hs 123 A-1; coded L2+JM of 4.(Schl.)/LG 2, Zalesie airfield, Poland, September 1939. The plane was finished in the standard pre-war scheme consisting of splinter patches in RLM 61 *Braun* (brown), RLM 62 *Grün* (green) and RLM 63 *Grau* (grey) on the upper and side surfaces, and RLM 65 *Hellblau* (light blue) on the underside. The unit's badge was painted on the forward fuselage.

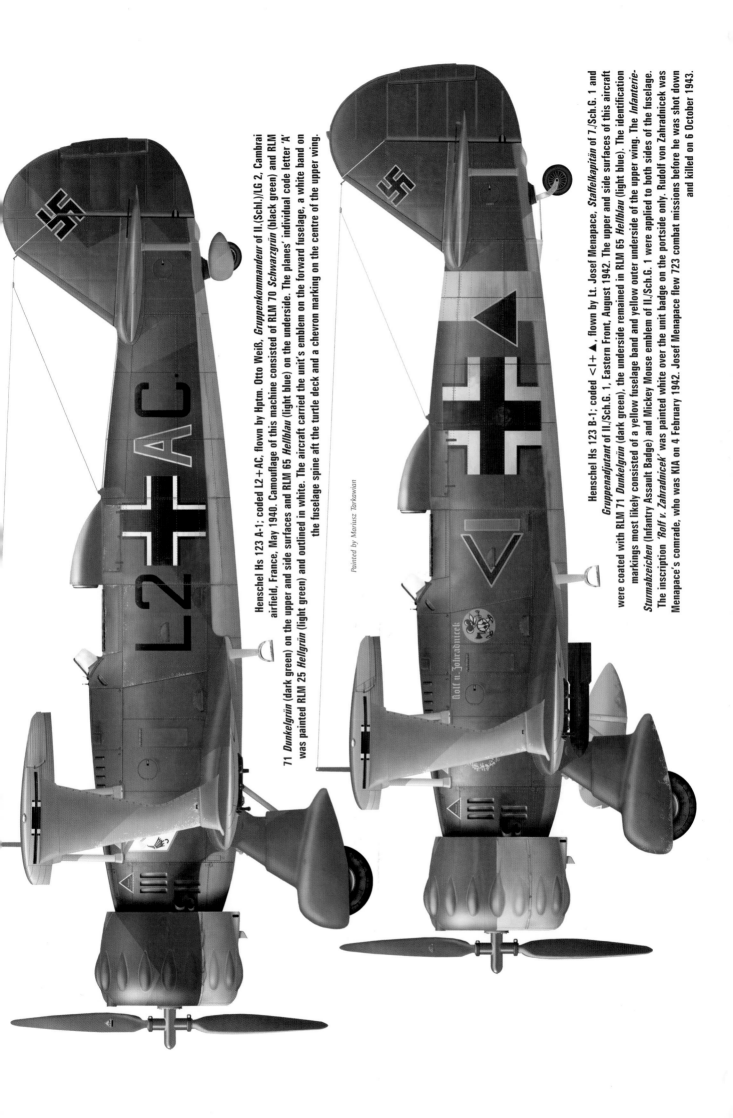

Henschel Hs 123 A-1; coded L2+AC, flown by Hptm. Otto Weiß, *Gruppenkommandeur* of II.(Schl.)/LG 2, Cambrai airfield, France, May 1940. Camouflage of this machine consisted of RLM 70 *Schwarzgrün* (black green) and RLM 71 *Dunkelgrün* (dark green) on the upper and side surfaces and RLM 65 *Hellblau* (light blue) on the underside. The planes' individual code letter 'A' was painted RLM 25 *Hellgrün* (light green) and outlined in white. The aircraft carried the unit's emblem on the forward fuselage, a white band on the fuselage spine aft the turtle deck and a chevron marking on the centre of the upper wing.

Painted by Mariusz Turkawian

Henschel Hs 123 B-1; coded <I+▲, flown by Lt. Josef Menapace, *Staffelkapitän* of 7./Sch.G. 1 and *Gruppenadjutant* of II./Sch.G. 1, Eastern Front, August 1942. The upper and side surfaces of this aircraft were coated with RLM 71 *Dunkelgrün* (dark green), the underside remained in RLM 65 *Hellblau* (light blue). The identification markings most likely consisted of a yellow fuselage band and yellow outer underside of the upper wing. The *Infanterie-Sturmabzeichen* (Infantry Assault Badge) and Mickey Mouse emblem of II./Sch.G. 1 were applied to both sides of the fuselage. The inscription 'Rolf v. Zahradnicek' was painted white over the unit badge on the portside only. Rudolf von Zahradnicek was Menapace's comrade, who was KIA on 4 February 1942. Josef Menapace flew 723 combat missions before he was shot down and killed on 6 October 1943.

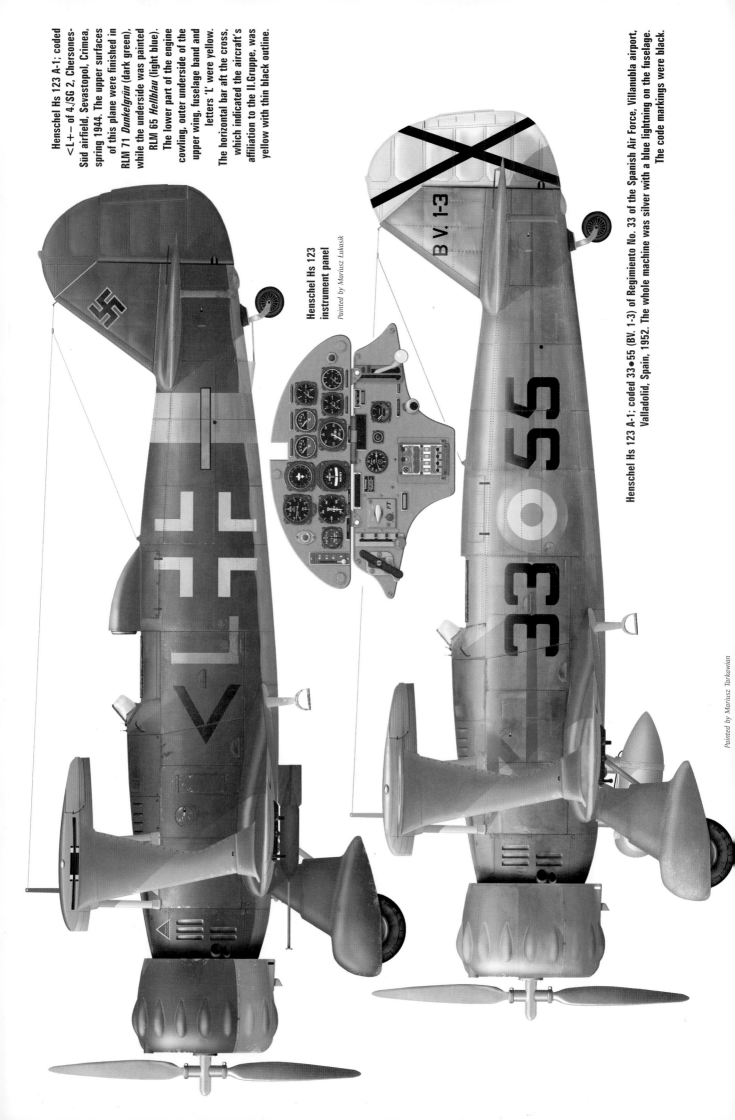

Henschel Hs 123 A-1; coded <L+− of 4./SG 2, Chersones-Süd airfield, Sevastopol, Crimea, spring 1944. The upper surfaces of this plane were finished in RLM 71 *Dunkelgrün* (dark green), while the underside was painted RLM 65 *Hellblau* (light blue). The lower part of the engine cowling, outer underside of the upper wing, fuselage band and letters 'L' were yellow. The horizontal bar aft the cross, which indicated the aircraft's affiliation to the II.Gruppe, was yellow with thin black outline.

Henschel Hs 123
instrument panel
Painted by Mariusz Łukasik

Henschel Hs 123 A-1; coded 33●55 (BV. 1-3) of Regimiento No. 33 of the Spanish Air Force, Villanubla airport, Valladolid, Spain, 1952. The whole machine was silver with a blue lightning on the fuselage. The code markings were black.

Painted by Mariusz Tarkowian